# NAZI ROCK STAR

## Ian Stuart - Skrewdriver Biography

## Paul London

© 2015 Midgård Records AB
Box 8, Alingsås, SWEDEN
info@midgaardshop.com

www.midgaard.org

ISBN: 978-91-982909-0-5

# Ian Stuart
# Nazi Rock Star

## Paul London

Thanks to: The producers of this book for making it a reality in print.
Everyone that helped with information and photographs.
Anyone that donned Skrewdriver's blackshirts and made Rock'n'roll history.

Special Thanks to AB.

Mighty Thanks to the big guy and his girl for their faith and courage.

# Contents

| | | |
|---|---|---|
| The Main Cast | Band Members 1977-1993 | 5 |
| Introduction | Paul London | 6 |
| Chapter One | Where's it gonna end? | 8 |
| Chapter Two | "I want to do this" | 11 |
| Chapter Three | Backstreet kids | 14 |
| Chapter Four | 1977 - The Year of Punk | 19 |
| Chapter Five | Built up, knocked down | 27 |
| Chapter Six | Turn of the Skrew | 37 |
| Chapter Seven | White Power 1,2,3,4 | 45 |
| Chapter Eight | Voice of Britain | 51 |
| Chapter Nine | All Hail the New Dawn | 57 |
| Chapter Ten | Behind the Bars | 62 |
| Chapter Eleven | Media Madness | 68 |
| Chapter Twelve | Strangers to the Truth | 71 |
| Chapter Thirteen | We are White Noise | 74 |
| Chapter Fourteen | Blood and Honour | 78 |
| Chapter Fifteen | False Dawns and New Horizons | 86 |
| Chapter Sixteen | Against Reds and Reaction | 92 |
| Chapter Seventeen | Nazi Chic | 96 |
| Chapter Eighteen | Reich n Roll | 105 |
| Chapter Nineteen | Out in the Cold | 112 |
| Chapter Twenty | Free my Band | 119 |
| Chapter Twenty-One | Betrayed | 125 |
| Chapter Twenty-Two | Waterloo sunset | 130 |
| Chapter Twenty-Three | 1992 - The Year of Treachery | 137 |
| Chapter Twenty-Four | Under the Cosh | 145 |
| Chapter Twenty-Five | Time to die | 149 |
| Chapter Twenty-Six | Aftermath | 156 |
| Discography | Skrewdriver/ Solo/ Klansmen | 161 |
| Index | A-Z | 163 |

# The Main Cast

| | | |
|---|---|---|
| Ian Stuart | Singer | 1977 - 1993 |
| Grinny | Drummer | 1977 - 1978 |
| Phil Walmsley | Guitar | 1977 - 1978 |
| Kev McKay | Bass | 1977 - 1980 |
| Ron Hartley | Guitar | 1977 - 1978 |
| Garry Callendar | Bass | 1978 |
| Mark Radcliffe | Drums | 1978 - 1979 |
| Glenn Jones | Guitar | 1979 - 1980 |
| Martin Smith | Drums | 1979 - 1980 |
| Geoff Williams | Drums | 1982 - 1984 |
| Frenchy | Bass | 1982 - 1984 |
| Mark Neeson | Guitar | 1982 - 1984 |
| Adam Douglas | Guitar | 1984 - 1985 |
| Murray Holmes | Bass | 1984 - 1985 |
| Paul Swain | Guitar | 1984 - 1987 |
| Steve Roda | Bass | 1985 - 1986 |
| Scotty | Drums | 1984 - 1987 |
| Merv Shields | Bass | 1987 - 1989 |
| Jon Burnley | Drums | 1987 - 1991 |
| Martin Cross | Guitar | 1987 - 1988 |
| Ross McGarry | Guitar | 1988 - 1989 |
| Smiley Jon | Bass | 1990 - 1993 |
| Stigger | Guitar | 1990 - 1993 |
| Mushy | Drums | 1992 - 1993 |

# Skrewdriver 1977 - 1993

# Introduction

It was as a fourteen year-old Skinhead irchin that I first met Ian Stuart. The venue was the Last Resort Skinhead shop in East London. Mickey French, the shop owner, was doing his best to hype up the return of Skrewdriver - *the* original Skinhead band. 'Strength thru Oi' was on the the shops turntable, booming out into the Sunday market, from strategically placed speakers the size of guitar amps. What struck me most was how approachable Ian Stuart was.

Courtessy of speaking to two guys, who looked like something out of a Charles Dickens novel, known as the twins, I was able to attend the 'Back with a Bang' return gig at London's One Hundred club. As well as working at the Last Resort, the two were also on duty at the door of the club - and whilst doing my best to look eighteen I would have never got in without them recognising me from the Resort.

I had been to gigs before, and while they too had been filled with racist Skinheads - this was something else. Instead of playing down the politics of those assembled before him - to the contrary Ian Stuart publicly encouraged it. Where bands like The Business and the Four Skins felt embarrassed - it was something Skrewdriver thrived on. For years of Skinhead groups watching their words, Skrewdriver were now saying what they wanted with a two finger salute to anyone who dared to argue.

Over the preceding years It was not only the music that I grew to know, but the man himself. His enthusiasm and character was infectious. He truly did make you feel that there was a purpose to it all. That one day we would win.

From a purely Skinhead point of view it was totally refreshing. Skinheads had always been racist to some degree or another, but the politicians of the right had viewed them as an embarrassment or front line cannon fodder. Here was a guy just like the other Skinheads, with a respect for his bootboy brethren. And for the first time it felt like they were calling the shots.

Most groups would have fallen at the first hurdle if they had faced the highs and lows of Skrewdriver's first venture into rock'n'roll in the heady days of Punk in the mid seventies. If anything it actually strengthened Ian Stuart's appetite.

The second boom between Nineteen eighty-two and Nineteen eighty-four was amazing in that we were witnessing a system in total shock. The electrifying power of Skrewdriver playing live was lighting up a music world that was swamped with mediocre bland songs and singers. And when White Noise records cut its first vinyl - the waiting world certainly wasn't ready for White Power.

The next real era of prominence came between Nineteen eighty-seven and Nineteen eighty-nine when Skrewdriver threw off the shackles of the National Front and started up the more radical Blood and Honour organisation.

All through the turbulent years of Ian Stuart's career he never lost his sense of purpose, or his sense of humour. Those who were fortunate enough to share a drink with him would, no matter what their political leaning, tell you what good company he was.

In the Rock Against Communism scene throughout the world Ian was respected and admired. Never once was he in danger of losing his throne, but yet to meet him you would find a level headed guy, unselfish and charming with it. There were of course other bands on the arena who were more than proficient in what they did, but they seemed happy with the status quo. It was a unity of ideals, one in which the other bands were always going to be fighting for the number two spot.

As the world closed its doors to RAC so the movement created its own identity and fiercly defended it. The downside of this was found in record reviews in the various Skinhead fanzines. Because it was felt that to even get this material released was such an immense achievement they felt compelled to rate everything ten out of ten. To criticise would be to betray.

For this reason I expect those still active in the scene to be uncomfortable with some of the contents of this book. I have set out to record events exactly as I see them. I see no need to sugar coat anything. In a fantasy world Ian Stuart rode a charriot of gold shooting Communist-crushing bolts from his swastika shaped guitar. In reality Ian Stuart was a uniquely talented and courageous man. But not everything he touched turned to gold, for instance some of the recordings made in his latter days were somewhat sub-standard in comparison to the quality he produced in the mid-eighties, but the good by far out weighed the average.

Whatever you think about this book I hope you will realise that it is a story of great importance in the history of Rock'n'roll and rebellion. There is no other agenda with this book other than to tell the story as it is.

**Paul London**

**The Truth Shall Set You Free.**

# Chapter One
# Where's it gonna end?

Born on Sunday the eleventh of August Nineteen fifty-seven, Ian Stuart Donaldson began life in Carleto, a quiet Blackpool suburb. Carleton is situated just a few miles from the bright lights of the golden mile, Lancashire's most popular sea front. The Donaldson's, who partly descend from Scotland, owned a tool making business. This enabled them to live in a three-bedroom semi in an affluent part of town.

Living just two doors down from the Donaldson's house in Hawthorne Grove were the Grintons. Their son John became friends with Ian at the early age of two. The pair went on to share many adolescent adventures together.

Ian's parents were strict and were incessantly concerned about his education. At one point they pulled him out of the Junior school he attended with John Grinton, in favour of one with a higher success rate.

Ian had a happy childhood. Much of his time was spent teasing his younger brother Tony. Mum and Dad would often come home to find that he had locked Tony in the coal shed, or was frightening him with ghost stories.

Attending Baines grammar school, Ian managed to collect five high grade O'levels. There was no doubting his intelligence, but his heart always tended to be in music and youth culture. On one occassion, when he failed an exam, his parents insisted he take extra tuition. John Grinton's parents seemed more easy going, although they were also keen to see John do well.

John's father had been in a band and both parents were keen to encourage John with his interest in music. It was there that Ian got his first taste of pop music. At the time the Beatles were riding high in the charts and were popular with almost all the kids at school. Ian found his first musical footing elsewhere. Mesmerised by the sight of the Rolling Stones performing 'Jumping Jack flash' for the first time on Top of the pops. It was their Rock'n'roll rebellion that really caught his eye. The two boys would often listen in awe at records by the Stones and The Who.

As he grew up, Ian began to get involved in fights. On a visit to Switzerland with the Cub scouts, he even managed to get into a fight with an American boy at the Scout camp. The news certainly didn't please his parents, but it was quite normal for boys his age to get into scrapes. Ian enjoyed fighting and became good at hitting hard and ducking the blows, unlike his chum John who seemed to continually return home with black eyes and bruises.

If he wasn't fighting or listening to Mick Jagger's vocal offerings, Ian would be playing football. Ian was a keen Manchester United fan as a child and like most kids wanted to emulate his heroes. Grinny went to Blackpool matches with his Dad and sometimes Ian would get to come along too. At a game where Blackpool were playing against Blackburn, Ian, a bit bored with the events on the field, started picking up bits of grit and throwing them at another lad. Eventually the lad got a bit of grit in his eye, and Grinny's Dad had to step in to stop the lads' older brother from throttling the young Donaldson.

Ian received a lot encouragement with his football and even had trials with Blackpool Football Club. Soccer soon made way for youth culture and he eventually stopped supporting Manchester United when they played Reme Moses, the first black player to wear a United shirt. A resentment of foreigners existed even back then.

When Skinheads hit the headlines in the early Seventies, John (known commonly to his friends as Grinny) got himself some boots and cropped his hair. Ian knew his parents would not allow him to do the same and so had to find other ways of assuming the style he so wanted to adopt. Opportunity knocked when he salvaged some old Steel capped boots that he pulled out of a School bonfire. His Grandfather gave him the money to crop his hair. Although probably not realising the consequences, he certainly approved of grandson's clean cut image. This, after all, was the age of Hippies and 'flower power'.

Ian bought a copy of the Richard Allen novel 'Skinhead' and read it from cover to cover. The book was set in the East end of London, and based around the life of fictional racist Skinhead Joe Hawkins. By day Hawkins would earn a wage delivering coal, by evening he was terrorising the streets with his Skinhead gang. As in real Skinhead tradition Bank holidays would see Hawkins and his fellow East London Skins set off for the sea-side to wage war with Bikers, Mods and anyone else who wanted it. Beating up Hippies and going on jaunts of 'Paki-bashing', Hawkins was the Skinhead born out of tabloid infamy. Most Skinheads didn't care just how stereotypical it all was, they loved it. The popularity of the paperback saw over twenty off-shoots including 'Skinhead return', 'Suedehead' and 'Dragon Skins'. The whole range earned Mr Allen a small fortune, and catapulted Joe Hawkins into Skinhead mythology. Ian drew great inspiration from the book, reading it over and over again.

Ian's parents were unhappy about the whole situation. In an attempt to stop his association with John, a neighbourly dispute began between the Donaldson's and the Grinton's. Both neighbours were blaming each other for their sons' behaviour.

The two boys friendship remained strong and now into their teens became more submerged in the Skinhead culture that had gripped Blackpool. There were venues playing Skinhead music, mainly Ska and Blue beat records performed by West Indian groups. Symarip's LP 'Skinhead Moonstomp' was very popular with the local Skinheads. This was partly because the record cover featured a picture of Tash Ashford and the Central Skins, a major Blackpool crew. The album became a Skinhead classic and remained so for many years to come.

The Skinheads had a notorious reputation for violence. They did have a 'them and us' attitude, but the fact that you were a fellow Skinhead certainly did not always ensure your safety. Gang rivalry was widespread. In the vicinity of Blackpool alone there were North shore, South shore, Central, Carleton and Poulton Skinhead crews.

Summer holidays were often spent fighting other lads from Poulton. Poulton's crew was much stronger than the 'Carleton firm' and was headed by Ron Hartley, who would later play guitar for Skrewdriver. Ronnie had a reputation for being tough and not many people in the area were prepared to take him on. Rucks normally took place on Carleton park. It was not a pretty sight, but never resulted in anything more than a few cuts and bruises and the odd black eye.

When the Skinhead craze died down Ian turned to the Suedehead scene. It was a natural progression. The new scene was made up mostly of ex-Skinheads who had out grown their crops and were listening to Northern Soul music. Lancashire was the capital of Northern Soul and every weekend the dance halls would blast out tunes by the likes of Edwin Starr and Melba Moore. Very much in the direction of the Mods, it had become the new fashion in the North of England and Ian found himself attending 'all nighters' at the famous Wigan Casino.

For Ian transport became a trendy Lambretta scooter. Although he had embraced the Ska and Northern Soul music of the Skins and Suedes, his main musical influence remained the Rolling Stones. Impressed by their style and attitude, he eagerly bought every record they released.

# Chapter Two
# "I want to do this"

At the age of sixteen Grinny had taken up his place as drummer in local band Warlock. Although very young, they still managed to get a residence at the Alpine club and regular gigs in Poulton town centre. Joining Grinny in the band were Anton Rosenfeld, Adrian Hildell and Phil Walmsley. Their set mainly consisted of cover versions of the Stones, Led Zeppelin and Bad Company songs.

One Saturday Ian ventured along to watch the band play live, he was impressed by the set-up and the girls who were keen to befriend the group. So taken back was he that when they came off stage he said to Grinny "wow, fuckin' hell, I want to do this." At the time Ian was working as a coach trimmer and desperately needed something else to fulfil his aspirations. He persuaded Grinny to get Phil Walmsley to teach him to play the guitar. He was quite jealous of Grinny's new found fame. Quickly picking up the guitar, he soon started writing his own material.

Towards the end of Nineteen seventy-five, Warlock split-up. Hearing the news, Ian wasted no time in approaching Grinny and Phil with the proposition of getting a new band together. With the addition of Kev and Sean Mckay, who he had known from school, the group was formed.

The new band's repertoire was dominated by Rolling Stones songs. When naming the group they also took inspiration from the Stones - adopting the monicker Tumbling Dice - the title of a Stones record. They played a couple of songs by the Who and Free with some original material thrown in for good measure. At the time it was common for Pub bands to play cover songs all night. Tumbling Dice soon became popular around the Poulton area.

After a while Grinny became side tracked with girlfriends and the like, frequently missing weekend rehearsals. This angered Ian who was working particularly hard at making something of the group. Grinny was sacked and the two friends fell out. A replacement was found in the form of a local lad called Steve Goulter who gladly took up the sticks. Meanwhile Grinny returned to the remainder of Warlock, and, with the help of guitarist Huey Beck, managed to get them back on the road.

Things were going pretty well for Tumbling Dice, so a rough demo was cut and Ian set about forwarding the tapes to various record companies. He soon found himself pleasantly surprised to receive an invitation to join a record label in London. It would inevitably mean a move South but it was something he felt prepared for.

Ian was delighted, after only a short while writing songs and playing gigs here he was on the tip of something big, or so he thought. He rushed around to see the rest of the group and tell them the good news. They were all very pleased, but it wasn't long before some of them started airing their doubts about the move.

Steve Goulter wasn't prepared to leave his girlfriend and Sean Mckay had no intention of dropping his plans to go to University. Absolutely deflated Ian could see that it just wasn't going to happen, with that the band split.

Knowing that he wouldn't have had that problem with Grinny, Ian set about restoring relations with his lifelong pal. He turned up at Grinnys and said, "Fucking hell, the wankers, I got them a record deal. Would you move to London? Steve wouldn't leave his girlfriend and Sean wants to be a student. That's it, I've packed the band in, I've crashed it. They are just not committed. I don't know what I'll do now."

This was Ian's first real taste of defeat. What worsened the feeling was the realisation that it was not through lack of talent, in fact it was quite the opposite. Opportunity had knocked and found that his was the only door opened to greet it.

A few weeks after the split, in mid-July Nineteen seventy-six, Ian and Grinny ventured to the Lesser free trade Hall in Manchester to see the Sex Pistols play. It was one of the first Punk gigs in the north of England. Supporting the Pistols were two local bands, Slaughter and the dogs, and playing their first show, The Buzzcocks. Malcolm Mclaren was strutting around in a wild suit, while the Pistols were going down a storm on stage. There was a buzz in the air, this was the happening place to be. The whole attitude of Punk was enthralling, the raw energy and aggression had never been done in such a way before.

Ian was captivated by it all. Without doubt Punk was where it's at. Bored with the mundane life of his Civil servant job at Warbreck hill, he asked Grinny to join him, Kev and Phil in making a new band. They immediately set about rehearsing new material. The new stuff was very much in the Punk mould, drawing their influence from such acts as The New York dolls, The Stooges and Patti Smith.

Again Ian had a record deal in mind, and so after months of rehearsing, the band set up in his father's workplace and recorded a rough demo. The sound wasn't too great, the noise from the amps was lost in the vast space of the factory, but it was a start.

Pleased with the general sound, Chiswick Records responded to Ian's letter that had accompanied the demo tape. Arrangements were made for one of their representatives to come up and see the band in Blackpool.

Chiswick Records was the brainchild of Ted Carroll, former manager of Irish rock band

Thin Lizzy and owner of the 'Rock on' record store based in Camden Town, North London. The label had been created in Nineteen seventy-four to deal in re-releases of rare Rock'n'roll singles. Carroll later moved onto producing records for bands that were on the edge of the commercial music scene. In the late seventies they produced some of the most important Punk and New wave bands around, such as The Damned, Count Bishops, Johnny Moped and Motorhead. Being a small label reaching the charts with their products was never their immediate intentions and some of their production methods often hindered any such chart success. Their first release was a single by the Count Bishops that cost just one hundred and sixty pounds to make. "When we set up it was without the idea of having hit records. We won't put out bad records just because they sell," said Ted Carroll. "Our main objective is to put out a good record and one we believe in."

Roger Armstrong met Ian and the band in Blackpool. After watching them blast through various covers by Patti Smith and the New York Dolls along with some of their own material he offered them a recording contract. They now needed a name for the group, and so Chiswick sent up a list of possibilities. Ian chose 'Skrewdriver', spelt with a 'k' for added effect. And so the legend of Skrewdriver was born.

# Chapter Three
# Backstreet Kids

*Backstreet kids, no future in sight*
*Backstreet kids, can't see no light*
*Backstreet kids, no money too*
*Backstreet kids, well what you gonna do?*
*'cause you're the Backstreet kids, Street rats*

Skrewdriver made their first live appearance in February, Nineteen seventy-seven, supporting French act Lil' Bob Storey, at the Manchester polytechnic. It was the first time the lads had unleashed their new Punk act and it met with a great reception, having to appease the requests for an encore, twice. Ian had found a new confidence and unlike his days with Tumbling Dice at the Norbrech Castle, he spent the whole gig without his back to the audience.

After the success of their first gig, the band ventured to London for the weekend to record a single for Chiswick. On arrival in London they met up with Roger Armstrong who took them to a gig featuring three Chiswick bands. The Count Bishops, The Gorillas and Lil' Bob Storey were playing at the North London Polytechnic.

The next stop was the Riverside Studios near Hammersmith, where Roger helped produce their debut single. 'You're so dumb' was a tirade against drugs. It was a brave contrast for a new band making its way in a music industry so predominantly in favour of the use of drugs.

*I'm just trying to get through to you, I'm not telling you what to do,*
*If you don't keep away from valium, I think you're stupid, You're so dumb.*

This was Punk with a conscience. "It didn't make us too popular in certain circles." Ian said later recalling the time. "They thought we were thickoes from a northern town talking about something that was quite hip to do."

The flip side of the single featured a raucous track 'Better of crazy', not a classic, but a fairly impressive debut for the young band. On its release, the single featured a photo of Skrewdriver on Blackpool beach, the famous tower a visible backdrop.

Everything appeared to be going in the right direction and Ian found that the local press in Blackpool were taking notice of the group. He told them that he started the band through boredom of his work in the Civil service, and that the Sex Pistols had been a major influence. Although the band had yet to play locally in the Blackpool area, this publicity bore witness to a growing home-based support for Skrewdriver.

The whole band were pleased with the result, seeing the first white label copy and finally realising that they had something on vinyl. It felt great, although Ian was particularly embarrassed if they went to a club and heard it playing. It was strange that a band's front man was so self-conscious. Even while recording the vocal tracks, Ian insisted on moving the other members of the band be out of his view.

On the ninth of April Music Week reported that Chiswick had signed two new bands to three year worldwide record contracts. Joining Skrewdriver were Dublin newcomers the Radiators from Space. Chiswick felt a need to look outside London to find new bands. "We have searched further afield for fresh talent. This is because there are more record company A&R men than there are punters in the Roxy club these days." Said Carroll. "The general vibe seems to be that if it moves and has a guitar around its neck, sign it. We wanted to get away from that."

## Chiswick adds two more new wave bands

CHISWICK RECORDS has signed two new wave bands to three year worldwide contracts.

The groups are The Radiators From Space, based in Dublin, and Skrewdriver from Blackpool, and their signings represent a new move on the part of Chiswick. Explained Chiswick boss Ted Carroll: "We have searched further afield for fresh talent. This is because there are more major record company a&r men than punters in the Roxy club these days, and the general vibe seems to be that if it moves and has a guitar round its neck, sign it.

"We felt the only thing to do was to look around outside London to uncover new talent, and that is what we have done."

Both bands have completed recording their debut singles, and these will be rush released together within the next few weeks. Titles will be Television Screen by the Radiators From Space (S 101) and You're So Dumb by Skrewdriver (S 1?).

Meanwhile Carroll claims orders of over 7,000 in the first week of release of The Feelgoods Tapes album and is about to ship out an LP of rare rockabilly called Hollywood Rock and Roll. He is also planning a single release Dirty Pictures, by new band Radio Stars.

Before signing for Chiswick, the foursome had decided to use stage names. Many groups did it a the time so they could avoid paying tax and claim dole money. Each of them had different names. Ian didn't like Donaldson because he thought it didn't sound very

Rock'n'roll. Using his middle name Stuart as his surname appealed to him, a Keyboard player in the Rolling Stones was also called Ian Stewart, so he stuck with that. While the band were being introduced to Ted Carroll, Phil had been to the toilet and unbeknown to him the rest of the group had introduced themselves by their proper names. When Phil said "pleased to meet you, I'm Ronnie Volume," the rest of them burst into laughter. Ian was always pulling stunts like this. While on stage during a gig, Ian passed Phil his glasses just to embarrass him, as he never wore them while playing live.

Three weeks into the release of the new single, Chiswick boss Ted Carroll told Melody Maker of his delight with the seven inch and his belief in the band. "Skrewdriver is a band we like. They have had no press coverage and it is not yet available in the bigger stores, but more than four thousand copies have already been sold."

Skrewdriver made their debut on the London live scene on Saturday sixteenth of April at the Roxy club. Situated in Neal street, in the heart of Covent Garden, the Roxy had become a legendary Punk venue. Their appearance was almost cancelled when Drummer Grinny had to have five stitches to a wound on his thumb. He had received the cut from a rough piece of sheet metal at work. For the gig his fingers had to be taped up around the drum stick and so the show went on. He was not the only casualty that night. The Saxophonist of headlining act Johnny Moped jumped off stage and landed on broken glass. He was rushed to hospital with blood pouring down his leg. Skrewdriver certainly made their mark, and received favourable reviews in the network of Punk fanzines. One editor wrote "I was surprised to learn that this was only their second proper gig. When they went into Anti-social, it was obvious that they were going to work hard for the crowd. They shift and I felt terrific."

That May Chiswick promptly set about organising a short London tour. It was valuable experience for the Lancashire lads, and would put them in good stead for when they moved to London on a more permanent basis. Already they had secured a firm following.

At one gig in Putney, South West London, Skrewdriver supported The Police who had to borrow their PA system for what was their first headline slot. At the time The Police did not have a great gig following and Skrewdriver stole the show. Both groups had shared a drink or two before the gig as was common at Punk concerts. There was a certain comraderie present. One thing that Ian liked about being in a band was the fact that he could get into other band's gigs for nothing.

Before moving south, it was decided that it would be great to stage a farewell gig in the Blackpool area. A band stand in Stanley Park was a regular venue for open air entertainment. A good starting point for local bands, it seemed ideal for what they had in mind. Applications were sent to Blackpool council for approval, but met with great uneasiness from the councillors. A meeting was called to discuss the proposition. Punk in Blackpool was unheard of, but judging by record sales alone, there was certainly a demand for it.

Prior to the meeting, Parks director Fred Mathews spoke to the Evening Gazette. "Punk rock groups are the way out extremes, and while I have never seen one performing, it is well known that their material can be offensive. They attract a section of people that other park users may consider undesirable." Such snobbishness continued when Councillor James Blake called for a total ban on Skrewdriver.

## 'No' to punk rockers concert in park

ALTHOUGH Carleton punk rockers, Skrewdriver, were this week refused permission to stage a "farewell" concert in Stanley Park, the group are having no difficulty finding audiences in London.

Skrewdriver turned professional and moved to London earlier this month, co-inciding with the release of their first record on the Chiswick label.

The record features two original compositions, "You're So Dumb" and "Better Off Crazy," the first written by vocalist Ian Stuart and the other by Ian and lead guitarist Phil Walmsley.

"The lads have played all the name clubs in London including the Marquee, the Roxy and Dingwalls," said a record company spokesman.

"They are quickly establishing a firm following."

Before moving to London, Skrewdriver played in Manchester, but they have yet to be heard by local audiences. And that was the idea of the free concert in Stanley Park.

But on Wednesday, members of Blackpool's Attractions and Amenities Committee decided that the group's entertainment was unsuitable for the park.

The group was formed by Ian, a former Warbreck Hill civil servant, who lived in Hawthorne-grove, Carleton. The other three members are Phil, of Elder-grove, Poulton; Kevin McKay (bass), of Robins-lane, Carleton, and John Grinton (drums), of Hawthorne grove, Carleton.

John went to Hodgson School, the other three were at Baines Grammar School.

On Wednesday twenty-second of July the meeting of the Attractions and Amenities committee of Blackpool council took just five minutes to deliver an outright ban on the group. Committee chairman Raymon Jacobs commented that "on hearing the record (You're so dumb) I couldn't make out one word". His fellow councillor Malcolm Lord added "They are already banned by the BBC and anyone in their right mind would not want to listen to their music". The only alternate comments came from Councillor Edmund Wynne who replied "Who says everyone in this room is in their right mind? " He went on to warn that by banning the group they may be giving them the publicity they seek.

'No Punk in the Park' screamed the headlines of the Gazette, the paper that had covered the story from the start. Ian told them "We couldn't understand why they refused us permission to play a free concert in Stanley park, it was very petty of them." It may have given the band free publicity but would cost them dearly in their attempts to play for their home support.

On hearing the decision Chiswick said they would try to find another venue in the Fylde area. The adverse publicity made it impossible and the idea was eventually shelved.

The only positive thing to come out of the whole affair was the inspiration it gave to Ian. He wrote Too much confusion, a scathing attack on the Blackpool council.

All the Councillors in Blackpool, With their poxy parks, Why don't you fuck off,
You're much too old to persecute us, And just think about that local publicity huh?
Thank you.

At the time the sentiments hit home with many young people who felt that old folk didn't understand or want to understand them. It was all done in true Punk fashion and later proved to be one of their most popular songs from this era.

# Chapter Four
# 1977 - The Year of Punk

"We will make it because our music isn't all about speed.
We even do an acoustic number that is totally different
from anything the other bands are doing." - Ian Stuart, August Nineteen seventy-seven

After the fiasco of ' Punk in the Park' it became obvious that the next step would have to be a permanent move to London. It was the centre of Punk and any group worth its salt had to prove itself on the London arena.

With a handful of London gigs under their belts, June saw the band move to North London. Chiswick had arranged for them to stay at a house where Nora, a friend of the band's manager Effi, lived. She had two big dogs with her, it was a large untidy place that Ian christened 'The Dog Shit Palace'.

It was hardly good living and on a budget from Chiswick of twenty-one pounds a week, they soon found out that the streets of London were paved with many things, but certainly not anything resembling gold. With the Sex Pistols on a budget of twenty-five pounds, they were not alone in their poverty. On top of their twenty-one pounds extra cash could be earned from gig appearances and magazine shoots. In one such shoot for Bravo, a German magazine, they were told to go down the Kings Road in Chelsea and pick up some new clothes. At Shepperton Studios they shared a stage with the Sex Pistols. Unfortunately Kev McKay couldn't make it, so Steve Strange took his place for the photo shoot. Steve had been hanging around with the band since their arrival in London. The whole arrangement was very contrived but supplied the group with badly needed money.

For the next set of gigs Skrewdriver played with the likes of The Damned, The Police and Sham 69. All seemed fine, but if they thought they'd left their bad luck at home in Blackpool, then they were sadly mistaken. All the way through a gig with The Police in Putney there were rumours that gangs of Teddy Boys were coming down to 'do the Punks'. Ian and company thought nothing of it, back in Blackpool they had always got on well with the Teds. They were totally unaware of the ferocity of the London Punk-Ted rivalry. All that changed when, while packing their gear away, a gang of Teds approached. The gang were led by a black Teddy Boy dressed in a leopard skin drape jacket. The air turned nasty and the place

TAKE a 19-year-old civil servant, bank clerk, labourer and student and you've got Skrewdriver --Carleton's first "punk rock" group --whose single is released in a couple of weeks.

The record feaures two original compositions. "you're So Dumb" and "Better Off Crazy." the first written by vocalist Ian Stuart, and the other by Ian and lead guitarist Phil Walmsley.

You can expect the ballyhoo of London punk rock brought to the publice eye by the notorious Sex Pistols. But how does this scene fit into the calm of Carleton.

"We were pretty bored with work," explained Ian, a Warbreck hill civil servant, of Hawthorne-grove, Carleton. "We've been playing together for several months and saw the Sex Pistols four times, long before they hit the headlines with their behaviour.

"I sent a tape of our music to the record company and they came to hear us play. We've recorded the single and hope to do an album later and turn professional."

The group, who say they are influenced by the Rolling Stones, played their first "prestige" gig recently supporting French new wave band Little Bob Story, at Manchester Polytechnic.

Skrewdriver consist of Ian, Phil Walmsley (lead guitar), of Elder-grove, Poulton; Kevin McKay (bass), of Robins-lane, Carleton: and John Grinton (drums), of Hawthorne-grove, Carleton.

erupted with violence. Phil hid behind some bins and Kev jumped in the van with Effi, the bands' manager. Grinny got a drum stand smashed in his face and Ian was doing his best to fight off three Teds.

Grinny lost three teeth and had to go to Queens Hospital in Roehampton to have twenty-six stitches in his mouth. The next day they returned to Blackpool, as they often would, to touch base and enjoy the comforts of some home cooking. While the rest of the band were enjoying the pleasures of a brief break at home, Grinny was in agony after visiting the Dentists. The pain was immense when bits of broken teeth were retrieved from his gum. By the time Grinny's gum had recovered it was time to return to London.

Effi had got the band a headline slot at a seedy little place in Kings Cross called the Rat Club. On arrival they were surprised to see the other acts on the bill. There were dwarfs and strange dancers playing weird music. It was filled with Fringe Theatre people and everyone shared a mixed changing room, much to the amusement of Phil and Grinny. It wasn't the usual thing but again they got paid and had quite a laugh.

The band then received their first write up in the music press. Reviewing a concert they had played in Camden's Dingwalls, Julie Burchill tore them apart. "Skrewdriver's singer limited his terpsichorean attempts to a lackadasial shuffling from one foot to another, in the manner of a small child with a desperate desire to use the can." She wrote, "He (Ian) was wearing baggy white trousers with the legend Skrewdriver inscribed across the groin, and I sighed in resignation to realise that I would never have the knack of such arcane subtlety." Finishing off the article by calling the band "parasites," Ms Burchill pulled no punches in her vicious slating.

This was Ian's first taste of the music media's venom and right away he could see that you had no friends in the press, it was all about hype. It was generally regarded that most music journalists were failed musicians and it was an accepted practice to pile dirt on anything considered un-chic. Some people could do no wrong, some could do no right, and Ian and co. fell into the latter category.

The band spent the last day of June in yet more trouble. Skrewdriver were on the bill at The Music Machine club in Camden, along with Nine, Nine, Nine and Ireland's Boomtown Rats.

The Rats were backed by an Irish millionaire, everything seemed to have been gifted to them on a silver platter. Their debut LP was about to be released and they simply oozed bad attitude. Spending nearly all the pre-gig time getting their sound-check right and finalising arrangements with an American Television crew, they left no time for the other groups to rehearse. They did an eighteen-carat job of rubbing everyone up the wrong way.

Both support groups came on and went down really well, then The Boomtown Rats appeared and found a less than appreciative audience. This was a hard-core Punk crowd and they didn't appreciate the Rats brand of watered down New Wave Pop. On top of this Bob Geldof, later of Band Aid fame, was strutting around the stage impersonating Mick Jagger. This really annoyed Ian who at the time was talking with 'Big Vince', a hardcore Punk with a violent reputation. Ian told Vince to "deck that wanker Geldof." The audience had already started throwing bottles, but when Vince began to walk up the stairs to the stage, Bob Geldof thought he was coming up to join him singing. "Whack! " the next thing he knew, Geldof was knocked to the floor. A few minutes later the bouncers dragged Vince outside for a beating. Ian and a couple of the Skrewdriver crew joined in, in a futile attempt to help Vince. Ian was trying frantically to pull a bike from a drain pipe, to hit the bouncers with. As usual, Grinny came off second best when a bouncer threw him down some stairs, leaving his with concussion. When the Police arrived everyone scarpered.

Later that week Ian laughed, tongue in cheek, when he told the press that "It was nothing to do with the music, it must have been a misunderstanding."

A picture of the bloodied Geldof featured on the front page of the following weeks New Musical Express, it accompanied an article calling for an end to violence at Punk gigs.

Geldof recalls the night in his autobiography 'Is that it?'. "The atmosphere was foul, we could sense that even from a stage seventeen feet above the dance floor. The band on before us who were half skinhead, half punk, had been holding out about how awful I was and what a sellout the band were. Half-way through our set a character walked on stage and hit me very hard, twice. I staggered to the side and fell over a camera man." Geldof went on to say that he "found it ironic that the music press were now calling for the violence to stop, considering that they had played a large part in inciting the phenomenon."

Despite the setbacks and the violence, this was Nineteen seventy-seven, the year of Punk. The Sex Pistols were on Top of the pops, It was indeed an exciting time. There were gigs almost every night and Skrewdriver were on stage at least once a week and had become very popular, especially with the Skinheads that had latched on to their gigs.

One of the Skinheads regularly turning up was Grahame McPherson, a sixteen year old, better known as 'Suggs'. Ian would often go out drinking with his crew, the 'North London

Skinhead Elite', which consisted of Suggs, Chas Smash, Toakes, Chalky and most of the faces that appeared on the first Madness LP. Ian decided to give him a job as Roadie, there were no wages, but it meant that he didn't have to pay to get into gigs.

Suggs was living with his mum at the time, in a high rise block of flats off the Tottenham Court Road. He hated school and would hang around Skrewdriver's squat with a few others. Graffiti was sprayed wherever they went, mainly scrawling "North London Skinhead Elite" everywhere. As a joke they sprayed "Northern fuckers go home" near the squat. Ian loved the banter.

Suggsy had a certain charisma about him and even at sixteen it was obvious to those around him that he was going to make something of himself. Suggs became good friends with Ian. Being around the group gave Suggs ideas and became a major influence on him in his pre-Madness days.

About the same time, Ian was knocking around with Joe Strummer, who he first met at Punk hangout, The Cambridge pub in Central London. His first group, The 101'ers, had been on Chiswick, his current band The Clash were making it big with their own brand of Brixton Punk. They were managed by Bernie Roades, who although being quite dictatorial, had the money and contacts to push the group. They had maximum publicity and featured regularly in the music press. This sort of backing had eluded Skrewdriver, and Ian was beginning to feel a bit let down by Chiswick, who seemed totally unprepared to invest in their bands. Even groups that signed to Stiff records, a label of similar size to Chiswick, were being pushed with regular music press publicity.

The Skrewdriver's next bit of bad luck came when Ian and Kev ventured into town to see another band play at the Roxy club. On leaving the venue they found that their van, containing over a thousand pounds worth of their equipment, had been stolen. Ian told Melody Maker "We will pay for information leading to the recovery of our van and gear." No-one was forthcoming and the only glimpse they got of the van was when Phil noticed it drive past them in North London. It had been re-sprayed and was going too fast for them to do anything about it.

So with the grand total of eighty-two pence in their pockets they began to ponder their future.

Chris Welch summed things up in his Melody Maker column when he wrote "Bad reviews, Bans, extortion, robbery, assault and battery. Skrewdriver have accepted the challenge of the roughest end of the rock business. You have to admire their courage."

Chiswick came to the rescue and promised to hire them the gear they needed to continue gigging. After all that had happened Skrewdriver still refused to bow out.

Skrewdriver made their first Television appearance in a programme entitled 'The year of Punk' that was being made by Janet Street-Porter. A short Interview was arranged in a cafe in the Notting Hill area where they discussed playing in London and the trouble they had encountered with Teddy Boys. The following night at the Vortex club, after borrowing some gear from another band, they performed an impromptu set for the benefit of the TV cameras. The crowd went wild when Ian went off into a tirade of Ted bashing, before launching into the ever-popular Anti-social.

When it was screened on the twenty-fourth of September, Skrewdriver became public enemy number one with the London Ted fraternity. At the time there were frequent running battles between Punks and Teds in the Kings Road and around Sloane Square.

Punk was becoming full of poseurs and 'Stars' and, although he loved being front man in the band, Ian hated people who had a chip on their shoulder. He took pleasure in knocking them off their pedestal, literally. At one gig, Stix Smith, a friend of Ian's who played drums for X-ray spex, was being hassled by Iggy Pop. The obnoxious Iggy was preventing Stix from leaving the dressing room by outstretching his arm across the doorway. Ian saw what was happening and came busting through, Iggy objected and so Ian flattened him. Iggy was dragged away by his minders and given a line of Coke to calm him down. Ian thrived on situations like that but the downside was the bad reputation he and the band were getting. In an interview he did for Melody Maker, Ian was asked if Skrewdriver were a non-violent band, Shocking the reporter he replied "No, no, I actually enjoy fighting. Fighting was the only thing to do in Blackpool. There were no rock concerts, you had to travel to Manchester or Liverpool for that. Blackpool is for pensioners."

At a time when people were telling the group to distance themselves from their part Skinhead audience, Ian and the boys reverted to their Skinhead ways. Grinny got his hair cropped first and the others followed suit. They were fed up with the poseurs who were turning up and claiming they were Punks. The whole Punk thing had become fashionable and was losing much of its cutting edge. Some people were more interested in how many safety pins they could put through their noses than enjoying the bands' performances. Skrewdriver were perhaps showing a little naivety and un-beknowingly playing into the media's hands. Skinhead hair cuts and boasts of violence could improve your street cred but could also line you up as this years scapegoat.

Regardless of their new image Skrewdriver's popularity had hit a peak, they held the house records at the Roxy and the Vortex. Chiswick wasted no time in arranging dates for the recording of their debut LP.

Recording commenced at the Riverside studios and as with the You're so dumb session, it was engineered by Neil Richmond and produced by Roger Armstrong. Roger was heavily into Speed, but the band found him easy to get on with, although at times Ian wondered whether he knew what he was doing. The recording was over within a week, they had complied with the requests of Chiswick and recorded a full LP and two singles. It was decided that the LP would be first released with thirteen tracks and it would play at forty-five rpm as opposed to the regular thirty-three rpm. Later they would release a fifteen-track album at the usual speed. This is what they did although the fifteen track version was only ever available on the continent.

The first release would be a double A side single, Anti-social / Nineteenth nervous breakdown, and would go out in October. Following that by a few weeks would be the LP All

Skrewed up and then a month or two after that Chiswick would produce the band's third single Streetfight / Unbeliever. The Streetfight seven inch never made it past the planning stages, perhaps due to the bands ever increasing violent reputation or through Chiswicks growing disheartenment with them.

One band that was receiving more than their fair share of newsprint at the time were Skrewdriver's main rivals Sham 69. They too had begun to pick up a violent reputation, not because of anything the band had done, but more for the gangs of Skinheads that attended their gigs. They became known as the Sham army. Ian used to get on with a couple of members of the group, but had little time for their outspoken singer Jimmy Pursey. He would often stir things up between the bands by slagging Pursey. Ian later said of Sham's leader, "I saw Jimmy Pursey turn up at gigs wearing baseball boots, change into Doctor Martens for the gig and then change back afterwards, he was just posing." Posing he may have been, but, unlike Ian, he had become something of a darling boy with the music press.

With the recording finished, the band returned to Blackpool. Once back, Phil decided that enough was enough and promptly quit the band. He wanted to go to college and study. Being in Skrewdriver was preventing that, so a decision had to be made.

Ian swiftly recruited Poulton Skinhead Ron Hartley. Ron was a good guitarist and Ian was even more pleased with the fact that he looked the part. Phil was constantly taunted about his attire and was often referred to as 'the student'.

Back from Blackpool the band found themselves shuttled off to a farm in Peterborough. A week long stay had been arranged by Chiswick who had lined-up a couple of prominent tours with Hippy-style groups Sammy Hagar and The Pat Travis band. The idea was to get

Ian Stuart

# Skroodrivaa: awl thai need iza brane

SKREWDRIVER
'All Skrewed Up'
(Chiswick Records)***

CORR... LUVVA duck. Waass orl dis den. A noo record by a group called Skroodrivaa. On sale £2.50 annorl. Playze at 45 r.p.m. Carn't be had cunnit. Yeah, zrrll 'ave summa dat.

And I thought skinheads became extinct about seven years ago. Silly me.

Skrewdriver are one of those bands that have, disappointingly, fallen prey to the whimsical desires of a faceless public. Musically they are a very tight hard grafting band into playing punchy rock rhythms. Their choice of material though on all accounts is almost completely uninspiring. Sincere and honest they probably are. The writers of great songs they definitely are not. At least not on this showing anyway. It's the same old recurring themes that are currently hounding the punk rock syndrome into dogmas that are again the mainstay of the subject matter here. If you're into chasing your own tail then you'll love the lyrics to this. But then again if you are like that then you're probably the type that gets off on listening to rain falling on the roof.

The lyrical stance, the *attitude*, taken by Skrewdriver on 'All Skrewed Up' is just too available. Too easy to latch on to and call your own. It fails to throw down any challenge to the potential listener. For chrissake, it's predictable with a capital P.

'I Don't Need Your Love', 'We Don't Pose' (which must get the poorest title of the year award), 'An-Ti So-Cial', 'Too Much Confusion'. We've all heard it done hundreds of times before. Yes they do what they do very well. *Big deal*. I've heard it done better. Every closet rock star in the land has probably written songs about much the same. Y'know, boredom, frustration, anger, sexual fear/assertion.

If it wasn't for the fact that they do sound genuinely hung up about everything I would have accused them of being too contrived.

Because you see 'All Skrewed Up' really could have been so much better. There is no doubt in my mind whatsoever that Ian (vocals), Ron (guitar), Kev (bass) and Grinny (drums) rightly deserve their place up there alongside their contemporaries as far as sheer rockability is concerned.

Production wise Roger Armstrong does the boys and himself proud by successfully embellishing the very loud, rude sound they possess whilst maintaining a conflicting very raw 'live' feel to the recording. Ian's throaty singing is mixed a little too far down for my taste but apart from that there is a distinctive line of continuity upheld through out all 13 tracks. Which in itself is no mean achievement these days.

There is no way Skrewdriver can be written off yet. Not by a long chalk and certainly not so early on in the game anyway. Perhaps a quick reiteration of New Wave policies might solve a few of the problems.

They've got the brawn. All they need now is the brain. — MICK WALL

---

them to write new material and brush up on their set. Such a tour would portray Skrewdriver in a more positive light and could lead to bigger and better things for the Blackpool combo. In reality they didn't really get much done and on top of that Ian was beginning to have second thoughts about the appointment of Ronnie. With an unhealthy appetite for alcohol and a lack of personal hygiene that had earned him the unwelcome nickname of 'Dirty Doug', Ronnie was beginning to show his true colours. There was no doubting his ability as a guitarist. Under the influence of booze he had become a liability, making a hash of it on his debut with the band while headlining at the Roxy.

Chiswick required promotional material so the new line-up had their first promotional photo shoot and the contrast in styles was noted by the music press. Antisocial was released with a cover picture of the group as Punks, yet the music paper advertisements showed them as Skinheads.

The following extract of a review for the new single in Sounds magazine was typical of what the critics had to say.

"This is stupid, crass, crude and maybe even half-witted and I love it. It's exactly what happens when rock'n'roll is left in the hands of Borstal fodder. This is raw punk with absolutely no redeeming features, but guts, honesty and chutzpah."

The critical reviews had done nothing to quell the interest of Radio One's John Peel who had been playing You're so dumb for a while. On the seventh of October he played Anti-social for the first time and after many requests from listeners, contacted Chiswick to arrange for the band to record a session for his evening show.

On Wednesday nineteenth of October the Skrewdriver crew, including the young Suggs, ventured into Studio four of the BBC's Maida Vale recording complex. There to meet them was Malcolm Brown and Nick Gomm who between them had worked on recordings by the likes of Free, David Bowie and The Police. The recording went well and Ian was pleased that the added experience of the production team was positively affecting the outcome.

Tracks recorded in the Peel session were Streetfight, Unbeliever, The only one, and a new version of the latest single, Anti-social.

# Chapter Five
# Built up, knocked down

The night before the Peel session Skrewdriver played to a packed audience at The Vortex in Wardour Street, Soho. It was a big night for the band. Representatives of the Sammy Hagar band were there to see the group they were poised to tour with. Others there were John Peel and a host of other top names in the music business, including The Who's Keith Moon who was quite a fan of the group.

The curse of Skrewdriver was again present to snatch the opportunity away from the palm of their hands. Violence at the concert was fierce, chairs and tables were broken up and used as weapons and the fighting spilled out into the streets of Central London. The lads knew that it could only spell doom for them. Within the following few days, news came through that both the Sammy Hagar and Pat Travis tours had been cancelled. In many people's eyes it was the beginning of the end. Skinheads at the concert were the perpetrators of the violence. This was the year of the infamous Lewisham riot, where running battles erupted between the National Front and Left-wing demonstrators. Links between the NF and the bands followers was putting Skrewdriver's political persuasion into question. The music industry was beginning to get cold feet.

Skrewdriver met up with Chiswick staff to celebrate the Peel session that was broadcast on the twenty-eighth of October. The evening was one full of high spirits, but it was apparent that Chiswick were trying to think of a way to dig themselves out of the mess.

There were no ultimatums, but pressure was placed on the group, and Ian in particular, to condemn the right-wing Skinhead faction that had latched on to the band. This kind of reputation could finish the group.

Ian liked being a Skinhead, most of the Skinheads he was hanging around with were racist and he wasn't going to condemn them. Although he was in no way connected to any political party at this stage, he was probably as racist as many of them and often refered to black people as 'Conkers'.

From a commercial point of view there couldn't have been a worse time to release an LP, but in the first week of November All Skrewed up hit the shops. Selling at two and a half pounds, the album consisted of twelve original compositions plus a cover of The Who's Won't get fooled again. "I want all you Skinheads to get up out your seats, put your braces together and boots on your feet and give me some of that old Moonstomping." - These words were scrawled across the back of the LP, taken from the lyrics of Symarip's Skinhead Moonstomp. As well as their attack on Blackpool councillors in Too much confusion, the group vented their anger at authority in the pacey Government action. Track eleven, We don't pose, was a dig at the poseurs that had showed up on the Punk band wagon, the lyrics striking and direct.

> *Well you can tell the old set, too cool to clap,*
> *We're gonna cut through, the posing crap,*
>
> *Just 'cause we look different and we wear different clothes,*
> *Just 'cause we look different, we, well we don't pose.*

There were no surprises when the press gave it a rough ride, mocking their thug-like image with headlines such as 'Skroodrivaa - awl thai need iza brane'.

It wasn't all negative though, the NME's Roy Carr wrote, "In Ian, these Blackpool boot boys have potentially one of the best gravel throated vocalists to emerge this year, while Ron, Kev and Grinny give the listener the distinct impression that they would be better deployed on more adventurous chords and rhythms."

Reviewing the album for Sounds magazine, Mick Wall complained about the fact that Ian's vocals were too low on the final mix, he also wrote "There is no doubt in my mind that they deserve their place among their contemporaries as far as Rockabillity is concerned. There is no way Skrewdriver can be written off yet. They've got all the brawn, all they need is the brain."

Although the group were finding that there were not many venues that would consider housing them, the album sales were encouraging, advance orders surprising even Chiswick.

With the storm of the Vortex still hovering over them, Ted Carroll suggested that they "roll on back to Blackpool to let it all blow over." It's exactly what the lads did and Ian seized the opportunity to ditch Ronnie. He told Ronnie that the band would split and in the meantime started to search for a new guitarist.

The new year didn't bring any change of luck for Ian, when attending a Fairport Convention concert, was involved in a fight with bouncers and received a beating, needing thirty-two stitches in a back wound.

The roller coaster ride that had become the career of Skrewdriver continued. With a new line-up they were operational once more. Phil Walmsley was back and joining him on guitar was former Eager Beaver guitarist Chris Cummings.

Still avoiding London, the new line-up made their first venture into Europe, headlining at

# London ban on punk rock group

**by ROBIN DUKE**

ILL FATED Blackpool punk rock band Skrewdriver have been banned from London.

Founder member Ian Stuart said that about half the band's current tour had been cancelled because of the skinhead image of violence the recently reformed line-up still had.

"All the London bookings have been cancelled so about 15 dates had been wiped off the tour," said Ian.

"We were told that the only bands that clubs were not prepared to put on were the Sex Pistols, Sham 68 and us," he added. "In a way, it's quite flattering, but it certainly doesn't help out our bank accounts."

Despite the London ban — which is based on the band's earlier skinhead image and violence which erupted at some of their bookings — Ian says that Skrewdriver are still looking for a Blackpool booking.

"We are hoping to hire somewhere in Blackpool and there is talk of a booking at the Roundhouse in London," he said.

"I think it is very unfair that we are branded as a certain type of band just because of an image that was wrong in the first place and is certainly not true of the band as it stands at the moment," said Ian.

"We are still an aggressive band but we can't really be called punk any more — we are more blues influenced than we used to be but people still want to brand us with our former image," said Ian.

Skrewdriver ... violent image.

the Gibis club in Paris. Not unlike the Roxy, The Gibis was a sweaty place, and bands such as The Damned, who had played there in the past, found that they had to work extra hard to catch the imagination of the audience, who at times had seemed happier with the Punk disco that proceeded the live bands.

The foray about the groups Skinhead image was still rumbling on in London, Chiswick were constantly telling Ian that they would get nowhere as a Skinhead band. Music journalists wanted Ian to make a statement distancing the band from their Skinhead following, this Ian had tried hard to avoid.

In March Ian wrote an open letter to the New Musical Express in a bid to clear the bands name.

"I am writing this letter in an attempt to put a few things straight. Number one is that Skrewdriver are no longer a Skinhead band due to the increase in violence at our gigs. We also realise that as a Skinhead band our gig schedule would almost be non-existent due to the Skinheads' violent image."

Ian continued to say that he had many Skinhead friends and didn't mind who came to gigs. Stating that the band was making a conscious effort to stop the problem, he blamed the trouble on a small minority. Ian then went on to attack Jimmy Pursey who was still having similar trouble at his concerts.

"Another matter I would like to bring up is the fact that I keep reading about Jimmy Pursey telling everyone who wants to fight to go to our gigs. Skrewdriver would very much appreciate it if Pursey would keep the problems in his audiences to himself. We have got enough of our own."

Accompanying the letter was a photo of the group in Punk attire. The gesture was sin-

cere but received typical press cynicism.

Sham 69 had managed to appease the music industry by slating their audience in the many articles the music press were happy to make room for. Any band that found themselves in such a position were often hounded by the press. To redeem themselves they would opt for playing benefit concerts for the Anti-Nazi League, an organisation set up by the far-left Socialist Workers Party to counter the success of the National Front.

The dilemma was worse for Sham and Skrewdriver, because both groups had set themselves up as Skinhead bands and any move away from that would be seen by their fans as an act of treachery. On one hand you could conform and hope to make it big, while being seen as dumping on the very people that put you there in the first place. Another option was to stick to your guns and disobey the might of music industry opinion. Both groups found themselves stuck between a rock and a hard place. They would find no sympathy from a music press that was only too happy to see the groups swallowed up by a beast of their own making. No-one in the business could see the possibility of any long term commercial use for such bands, unless they were prepared to conform.

Signed to a major record label, Sham were more likely out of the two to make it big. The glare of the bright lights was too much for Jimmy Pursey and in the hope of fame and for-

tune he sold his soul to the music corporations. At least that's how the Skinheads saw it.

Before too long Sham had joined the long list of groups that had succumbed to the media pressure, by playing for the Anti-Nazi League. Sham appeared at a major Rock against Racism event in London. It was a deadly blow to the hordes of National Front and British Movement Skinheads that had followed Sham. It would be a compliment that the Skins were only to happy to return.

The violence continued, and Sham, with Jimmy pursey in tears, announced that they would be forced to call it a day if they didn't see an end to the trouble. For the next eighteen months they split and reformed on a regular basis. Each time they returned, so did the violence, culminating in a farewell show - Sham's last Stand, at the Rainbow theatre, Finsbury Park. It was all very predictable and just too much for Pursey to bare. He fled the stage in tears to the chants of "Sieg Heil" from over a hundred British Movement supporters in the audience.

Image wasn't the only thing that was changing within the Skrewdriver camp, with the short-term departure of Phil and Grinny, Ian recruited Garry Chammings to play drums. With a new manager, Johnny Quincy, and now based on the Wyre area, Skrewdriver moved away from Punk and headed for a Rockier and more melodic sound.

After missing out on the trip to Paris, Grinny returned to the band in preparation for their visit to Groeningen, Holland, where they headlined at a two day open-air Punk festival that also featured The Stranglers.

For Grinny it would mean leaving his job at ICI, a job that his father had pulled all the strings to get for him. Grinny later regretfully retracted his services, a blow that doubled with the crashing of the groups van a few days before they were due to leave. The line-up was going through regular changes. Ian pulled in Bolton drummer Mark Radcliffe who joined Phil on Bass, and Ronnie back in on guitar. Mark had known Phil from College and was keen to get into the music scene having had little success with his former band 'Ridiculous and Jones' that also featured Phil on guitar. In the end the curse of Skrewdriver reared its head again and the group had to endure a torrential rain storm during their Dutch performance. Hailed as "the most blistering live act in Britain" the concert was a total disaster.

Although it had been something of an eye opener for Mark Radcliffe, he decided to stick it out with the band a little longer playing regularly in Machester and as far afield as Leeds and Dunfries in Scotland.

Mark Radcliffe later surfaced in the Shirehorses and then on to broadcasting fame with his own show on BBC Radio One. Recalling his days with Skrewdriver in his book 'Showbusiness' he remembers Ian as "charm personified" before dissassociating himself with the band's future political leanings. To this day Radcliffe and Phil Walmsley remain

great friends.

Before being jailed for fraud, their manager Johnny Quincy secured the group some much needed gigs in the Manchester area. Their violent reputation had yet to reach Lancashire, and the band was again finding relative success on the live circuit.

Although there was still no sign of the third Chiswick single, Skrewdriver did however appear on a Compilation LP 'Long shots, dead certs and odds on favourites,' along with the likes of Motorhead, Radio stars and a host of other Chiswick signings.

Ten months had passed since their last London booking, so Chiswick set about arranging a nationwide tour. With their Skinhead look gone, it was hoped the band could recoup on lost ground and pave the way for their second album release on Chiswick.

Once again it wasn't long before doors started to close on the band. Venues had been warned about their reputation and were not prepared to take any chances, the music press laid a blanket of silence for the group.

"We were told that the only groups that clubs were not prepared to put on were the Sex Pistols, Sham 69 and us." Ian told the local press. "I think it is very unfair that we are branded as a certain type of band just because of an image that was wrong in the first place and is certainly not true of the band as it stands at the moment. People still want to brand us with our former image."

Out of a thirty-two-date tour, twenty-one were cancelled, mainly in the London area. It seemed that people in the music business had certainly marked their card.

Now based in Manchester, Ian assembled another new line-up consisting of Glen Jones on Lead Guitar, Gary Callendar on Rhythm, Kev McKay on Bass, Grinny on Drums and Ian as ever covering the Vocals.

The NME sent a reporter to one of the groups non-cancelled gigs at the Fforde Greene in Leeds. It was clear by her review that she had come with hatchet in hand. "Their tour having been wrecked by

the Skinhead reputation that proceeded them, the band (especially vocalist Ian Stuart) seemed anxious here to prove that they are a very dispensable act anyway." Ms Ruth continued, "For all I know, Skrewdriver could be genuine victims of the company they attract.

The method they employed here was truly kamikaze."

The new set failed to please the NME and also failed to delight Chiswick who sent Roger Armstrong up to Manchester as a prelude to recording the second LP. The new material that included Built up, knocked down, was a disappointment as far as Roger was concerned. Skrewdriver had left the Punk thing behind and with it they left any hope of further recordings with Chiswick. It was the final straw and indicated the end to their relationship as Grinny recalled. "They wanted the hundred-mile-an-hour Punk thing, but we were playing more melodic Rock stuff. It was a mutual separation. They hated the violence tag and the NF, we thought they were pro-IRA and Ian would always argue with Stan. Ian was pissed off with the way they did things. We should have been charting at the lower end of the charts. They pressed so many and it would be going well and then they would run out. Chiswick would then go back and press some more, but by then it had lost its momentum. They were frightened to put money into it. Ian was always dissatisfied with that."

Without a record company and living in rat infested dwellings in Salford, Manchester, Ian soldiered on. Gigs were frequent though and there was even talk of a Live LP to be record-

ed at Tony Wilson's, later of New Order fame, venue The Factory.

One day, out of the blue, Ian got a call from Chiswick asking if the band wanted to support Motorhead at the King George's Hall in Blackburn, they didn't need to be asked twice and promptly started organising things. Although they had let their hair grow, the only clothes they had was Skinhead apparel. Ian cut the sleeves off his denim jacket in an attempt to be more in tune with audience. On the night of the gig, some of Motorhead's equipment failed to turn up, so they had to borrow a Marshall stack and a couple of guitars from Skrewdriver. All went well and the two groups finished the night getting drunk together. Ian and Lemmy got on particularly well. Ian often used to go over to Lemmy's place to see him from time to time. Inside his flat he had a large propeller from a Meschershmitt hanging on the wall. Lemmy was into collecting old Nazi regalia.

Ian was often down in London, even managing to get the occasional gig. He was hanging around with Suggs a lot. Madness were just getting under way and the band would lend Skrerwdriver's gear from time to time. The music wasn't Ian's cup of tea, but he still showed his face at a few of their gigs.

About this time Grinny left Skrewdriver and joined The Nipple erectors, who became better known as The Nipps. They were signed to Soul records, a label that had employed various ex-Chiswick staff.

Fronted by Shane McGowan, (who later saw fame with The Pogues) The Nipps played some fairly big gigs supporting the likes of The Jam and went on to release a couple of singles.

Ian was eager to get some of his new material out on vinyl and so struck up a deal with Manchester's TJM records to release a single. The seven inch featured a line-up of Ian, Kev, Glen Jones and new drummer Martin Smith. The foursome recorded Built up, Knocked down, Breakout and A case of pride. The record certainly cast a new light on Skrewdriver's musical prowess, but unfortunately for the group, the music media totally ignored it. Perhaps it wasn't surprising considering the theme of the title track, Built up, knocked down, was a direct attack on the music business.

> *Quit my job and I went out, bought my first guitar,*
> *Then I started to learn a thing, Instead of propping up some bar,*
> *Sent a tape, got a contract, Made us all so glad,*
> *Then they started messing around with us, And now life's as bad,*
> *Are you trying to mess us up now, Trying to make us quit?*
> *If that's what you're trying to do, Well you ain't achieving it,*
> *Built up, Knocked down, Knocked down to the ground.*

Disillusioned with all that was happening with the band, Ian had started to get involved with the National Front. He liked being a Skinhead and could see nothing wrong with being patriotic. He was heavily influenced by a Lancashire Skinhead known as 'Scully of the East end', nicknamed so because he spoke with a dodgy Cockney accent. Ian had no love of Blacks and his experience with them during his time in London had done nothing to alter his feelings on the matter. Almost all the Skinheads he knew were that way inclined, so he joined up and it wasn't long before he was a leading activist in the Young National Front section.

Eventually Ian could see nothing coming of the band, so he decided to call it a day and return to Blackpool. As far he was concerned he could not see where he could now take the band, it was a decision that he made reluctantly.

It wasn't long before again Ian returned to London and stayed at a squat with Ron Hartley. He also spent more time with Suggsy. While in the capital, he was also knocking around with people from the London National Front. After much deliberation and discussions with the YNF leader, Joe Pearce, he said he'd consider reforming the band and join the newly launched Rock Against Communism.

RAC was formed as a direct response to the success of Rock against Racism. Ian said he'd play at their debut gig at Conway Hall in Holborn, but failed to show on the night.

Melody Maker sent journalist Vivien Goldman to check it out. The bands that played were White Boss and Dentist, two Punk groups who had nailed their colours to the post of RAC. Ms Goldman was told that Skrewdriver were supposed to play 'but had to bow out due to record company pressure.' This was the final nail in the coffin of Skrewdriver. Any commercial credibility they had retained had just gone out of the window.

In a vain hope of reversing the situation, Ian wrote to Melody Maker to complain.

"The biased information that appeared recently in your paper, and which RAR seem to be responsible for, is false. The news that Skrewdriver is reforming to do NF gigs is complete and utter bullshit. I have no interest in politics and never have. I've also been told that RAR has solid links with the Anti-Nazi League, an organisation who, it seems, are backed heavily by the Communist and Marxist parties, who in their way are just as much of a threat to this country as the NF or BM."

Ian went on to say that he was "forming a band that was not called Skrewdriver, and doesn't intend to do gigs for the RAR, NF or any other political organisation."

The Manor Park Royals was the group he was referring to. Ian hadn't lost his appetite for music and was keen to return to the stage, but would have to wait a little longer for his return as the Manor Park Royals project failed to get off the ground.

# Chapter Six
# Turn of the Skrew

"The National front is a Nazi front, Smash the National Front!" screamed one side of the road. On the other side endless streams of Union Jack flags were being marched along to the chorus of Rule Britannia. Skinhead Ian Stuart was among the latter.

Just as rock'n'roll had enticed him a few years earlier, politics of the Nationalist variety was catching the imagination of the twenty-one year old. The more he thought about it, the more he wanted to be involved. Ian never did anything in half measures, and politics was no different.

In Blackpool he joined both the British Movement and National Front and became a regular at National Front meetings. The meetings were held on Thursday evenings in an office above a garage and chaired by Alfie Hansen.

Attending the meetings with him was Scully, who had fed him with NF paraphenalia, and had become a major influence on Ian's political outlook.

Before too long Ian was appointed Young NF organiser for the area. Not content with that, his next ambition was to receive a gold badge. To qualify for the badge he had to recruit fifty new members. Ian dedicated a lot of his time to the task of persuading most Blackpool Skinheads to join up.

Ian's organising skills were coming to the fore in arranging newspaper sales and recruiting numbers for demonstrations. His most successful endeavour came when his branch attacked a bus load of IRA sympathisers on their way to a 'Troops out' demo. The bus was destroyed, leaving the occupants with various injuries, and the assailants got away without being arrested. Ian was indeed getting a name for himself as a hard-liner and a staunch activist.

If there was any reservation over Ian's political persuasion in the past, those who were in his vicinity now were left in no doubt. With no worry of the band's reputation to hold him back, Ian was totally unguarded about it. The Skrew had finally turned.

Ian hadn't cut all ties with London and, bored with the apathy of Blackpool, was again heading south. On arrival in London he received an invitation from Suggs to stay at his mother's flat. Suggs had moved out to a new house and the room was sitting empty. It was an offer that Ian gladly took up, staying there for over three months. With no Skrewdriver money coming in he needed all the help he could get. The DHS was his next step, Unemployment benefit would be his only steady income for the next while.

A little boost to his financial predicament came in the form of appearance money from the Bovver Boots film agency. Based in Leytonstone, East London, they were responsible for supplying 'tough guys' and crowd extra's for film sets.

In March Nineteen eighty-one Madness started filming 'Take it or leave it' - the story of their rise to fame in the pop world. Suggs suggested the opportunity of earning some extra cash and so Ian went along and signed up. When the film was finally edited and released Ian appeared in two scenes. In a fight scene he had to rush out of a toilet cubicle and attack the lads from Madness, playing out the experience the seven piece had faced when they played to a hostile audience at the Acklam Hall in Ladbroke grove, West London.

Ian soon dropped out of Madness activities after attending a prize giving show. He found it very contrived and thought the back patting was nauseating to the extreme. Despite everything, the two remained friends and Ian again returned to Blackpool to take up where he had left off with the Blackpool NF.

The stage had never been far from his mind and again he thought of starting a new group. He began to write new material, this time his lyrics were tinged with the patriotism that had so engulfed his soul. The hurt he felt at the hands of the music industry while with Skrewdriver was apparent and took up much of his writing subject. In one new song, If there's a riot, Ian quite clearly refers to that fateful night in October Nineteen seventy-seven, at the Vortex, which spelt disaster for the band.

> If there's a riot in here tonight, If you try it, in here tonight,
> If there's a riot in here tonight, That's bad news,
> You'll find yourself banned from everywhere,
> You'll find the criticism hard to bear,
> Keep a strong will, hold your head up high,
> Make sure Skinheads never die.

Ian toyed with the idea of forming a band called simply 'Britain', but in the end vied for resurrecting Skrewdriver. In July he told the local press in Blackpool that Skrewdriver would be backed by the National Front and would partake in a nationwide tour that September. He was premature in his hopes and again nothing came of it. He had felt let down by the NF who he thought would jump at the chance to cash in on Skrewdriver's re-birth. Not everyone in the racist party was keen on the type of music Skrewdriver

---

**Front behind punk group**

*10 JUL 1981*

THE Carleton punk rock group Skrewdriver is to re-form for a tour organised by the Young National Front.

Two of the original members and two newcomers will be playing a series of about 10 concerts in September and October — details of which are being kept secret "to avoid possible violence."

Founder member Ian Stuart, a former civil servant of Hawthorne Grove, Carleton, said the group — which in its earlier form was banned from a series of London bookings because of their skinhead image of violence — would also be trying to arrange a Blackpool booking.

The tour would include concerts in Birmingham, London, Manchester, Scotland and possibly Northern Ireland, he said.

"People at the clubs know they are National Front bookings," he added.

He and drummer John Grinton were National Front members, he revealed. The other members, Paul Higginbottom and John Pearce were joining "at this week's meeting."

Skrewdriver in the past have been banned from Blackpool's Stanley Park, had their equipment stolen and been involved in violent scenes after concerts.

Stuart dismissed suggestions that their re-emergence might be seen as inflammatory with the recent outbreak of inner city violence.

"This tour was arranged before the rioting," he said.

played. One NF leader referred to Punk as 'alien jungle rhythms'. Another Front publication labelled Sex Pistols vocalist, Johnny Rotten, a 'white nigger'. New wave was viewed by many older members as degenerate.

After being made redundant from his tool makers job, Ian again returned south and moved into a flat in Hackney, East London, before moving permanently to the Ferndale Hotel, Argyle Square in the heart of Kings cross. It was a Square that Ian would know as his home for the next eight years.

His choice of the Ferndale was not taken at random, Ian knew it well and often stayed there while on weekend jaunts to attend NF activities. The hotel was owned by Maurice Castles, an ex-National Front member who was only too pleased to welcome this new clientele.

With the addition of a few of Ian's friends as tenants, the hotel began to get a reputation as a 'fascist hangout' and before long Mr Castles felt the wrath of Camden council, who were very unhappy to learn the identities of their new residents.

The big news for Skinheads in Nineteen eighty-one was the riot in Southall. An Oi concert had been arranged in this predominantly Asian area of West London. On the bill were The Last Resort, The Business and The Four Skins. The inevitable happened and the Skinheads looked out of the Hanborough Tavern windows to see Asian youths mobbing up, first throwing stones and then petrol bombs. A police transporter bus was commandeered, set on fire and driven straight at the pub. Police fought running battles with the Asians, incensed at having their home town invaded by Skinheads. Although they were quick to condemn the Skinheads, the police were pleased to have their assistance when it all went off. The area had a history of racial conflict and even without the benefit of hindsight it was possible to forecast the events of that summer night. The Hanborough Tavern was burned to the ground and the East London band The Four Skins became the immediate scapegoats, even appearing on TV attempting, unsuccessfully, to clear their name.

Until that time Oi had been rising. It was very much a Skinhead based movement and had received a fair bit of help to get it off the ground from Sounds journalist Garry Bushell. Bushell had assembled two compilation albums released on the EMI label featuring Oi songs and poems. With Southall blasting everything into the open, Bushell quickly attempted to distance himself from one of the LP's, when it was revealed in the press that the cover model was none other than British Movement hard man Nicky Crane. The name given to the album 'Strength thru Oi', was a direct play on words for the Hitlerian slogan of the thirties 'Strength through joy', although this caused alarm, the actual record contained no trace of racism.

Ian could see a similar fate that Skrewdriver had experienced, awaiting the bands involved, and within a few weeks the Four Skins announced that they were unable to play anywhere and were splitting up. The Last Resort only lasted another six months by playing tightly arranged gigs. The Business attempted to clear their name by appearing in the music press with Asian Skinheads and playing a benefit gig for anti racist causes. It was a blatant play on tokenism, but some music journalists seemed to buy it.

Ian became a regular visitor at the East London Skinhead shop The Last Resort. Situated in the famous Petticoat lane street market, it had become a Mecca for all London Skinheads.

It was while at the shop that Ian was asked to reform Skrewdriver. The shop's owner Mickey French was prepared to back the group, and with the growing interest in Oi and Skinhead culture, he was assured that there was certainly a demand.

Mickey French had started off selling Punk clothes on a market stall, and, with the Skinhead boom of the late seventies, he started to carry Bootboy clobber. The change-over had proved fruitful and before too long he had moved in to Forty-three Goulston street. The shop was aptly named The Last Resort and a neon light eliminating the name was set up on the shop front. Inside the store you were welcomed by walls covered in the Resort's very own T-shirt line, exclusively designed by Skinhead artist Mick Furbank. Included in this line was the ever popular 'Crucified Skin' shirt, available with or without a Union Jack background. Behind the cash desk stood a six-foot model of Marilyn Monroe. Any Skinhead living within a hundred-mile radius would at some point feel obliged to pay homage to the only Skinhead shop in the World. They didn't particularly go for the wares on sale, many of which were poor quality, but to stand outside and chat with fellow Skins while Cock Sparrer, Last Resort and Strength thru Oi tracks boomed out of a giant speaker placed outside the shops entrance.

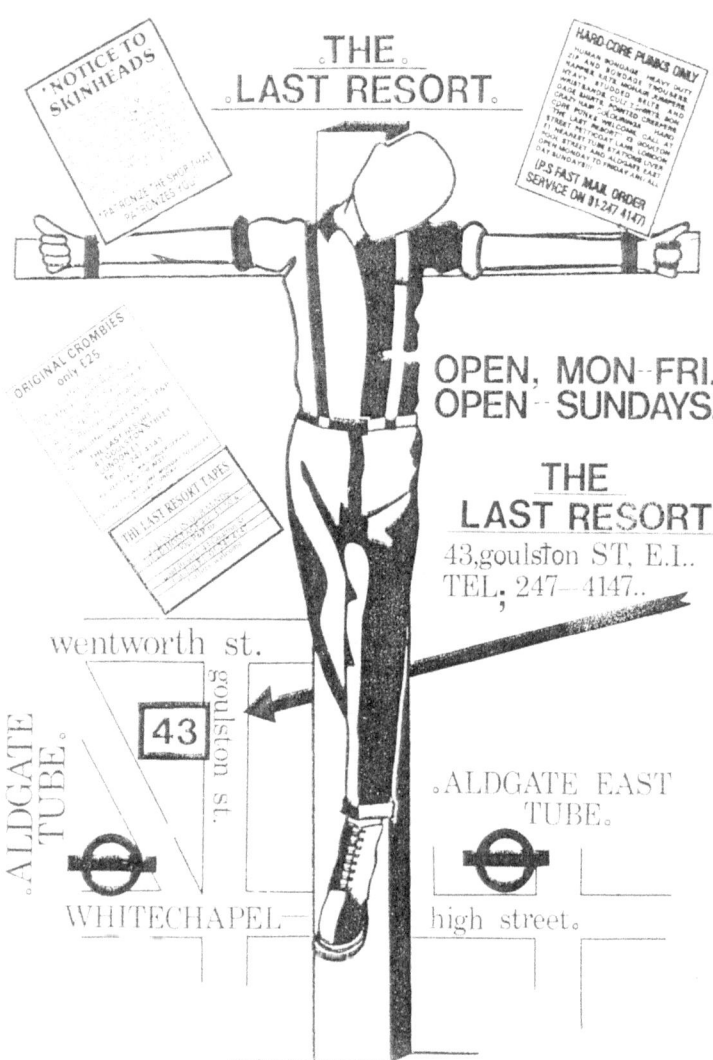

Market shoppers and tourists would glare as they went by, but surprisingly the shop had a fairly trouble-free existence. Mickey's wife Margaret was keen to prevent Skins from wearing Swastika badges and reading Bulldog by the shop front, and generally this seemed to be adhered to. The big day at the Resort was Sunday. Skinheads would come from all over London, stand around for half the morning before retiring to the local pub, usually the Apples and Pears in Liverpool Street train station or Dirty Dicks directly opposite the station.

Ian considered the possibilities carefully and, in the summer of Nineteen eighty-two, decided to start the band once more. His first job was to find a new line-up. There was no trouble recruiting his new bassist Mark French (Frenchy) and drummer Geoff Williams from the remnants of South London's very own racist Skinhead band, The Elite.

'Skrewdriver Needs YOU!' Screamed the advert placed in an August edition of Sounds magazine. The ad for a budding Skinhead guitarist promised a European tour and a record deal. The contact number given for Boots and Braces record company, was in fact the number for the Last Resort shop, who had already set up a line of Skrewdriver T-shirts.

Within days the vacancy was filled by Mark Neeson, better known as 'Lester'. Once again Ian's resilience had paid dividends and the words on everyone's lips were Skrewdriver are back.

With the help of Mickey French, the group went into the Workhouse studios in South London to record some new tracks. Two songs, Boots and Braces and a revamped version of Anti-Social, were recorded for a compilation LP called 'United Skins' and another two, Back with a bang and a new interpretation of the Nineteen seventy-seven song, I don't like you, for a new single. Both were to be released on the Boots and Braces label.

Back with a bang received a favourable review in Sounds, although the question of the band's political persuasion was again under the spotlight. Even though Ian was by then heavily involved in the activities of the National Front, he was reluctant to totally push it with the group.

*Do you remember in the summer?*
*back in Nineteen seventy eight,*
*When they reckoned that the Skinheads days were numbered,*
*And the papers dripped with liquid hate,*
*Being patriotic's not the fashion so they say,*
*To fly your country's flag's a crime,*
*Society's tried its best to kill you,*
*But the spirit lives until the end of time,*

Back with a bang became the Skinhead anthem of the early eighties and the Last Resort was doing a roaring trade in selling the twelve-inch single.

Skrewdriver's lyrics were certainly tinged with patriotism and it was this that was alarming the music press enough to adopt a cautious approach.

Ian attempted to cool the attention on the group's politics by speaking to 'Noise' magazine. "I said it once, but we never did it (Play for the NF). I was wrong. I don't want anything to do with fascism." Ian also wrote an open letter to Sounds.

"I read your review of Back with a bang in Sounds and it seemed fair, unbiased review. However, I cannot understand the necessity to mention fascism every time our name is brought up. Skrewdriver are not a political band, and none of us are involved in politics. I cannot understand where you get the ridiculous idea that anyone who wears a Union Jack is some sort of a Nazi!"

On the seventh of October Skrewdriver played their first gig in nearly three years, at the One-hundred Club on London's Oxford street. The gig was a prelude to the much publicised 'Back with a Bang' concert two weeks later at the same venue.

Both gigs went well and earned the group a regular slot at the One-hundred club. The set was pacey and made up with new songs, a few old punk numbers, a cover of the Rolling Stones' Street fighting man and Sham's Red London. The new material was a move away from the bluesy Built up, knocked down. It wasn't Oi but rather R'n'B influenced punk.

Nationalistic tracks, such as Don't let 'em pull you down, were indicative of where Ian was taking the band. Unpopular with the music press but music to the ears of the NF and BM Skinheads that made up most of Skrewdriver's audience.

*We're flying the Union Jack,*
*And there ain't nothing wrong with that,*
*We're flying the Union Jack,*
*And there ain't no turning back, White man,*

*Wherever you go, whatever you do,*
*You're always getting picked on, because you're red, white and blue,*
*The Judge is in the pocket of Mr Moneybags,*
*The others follow leaders and wave the red flag.*

Ian also doctored some of his old songs to represent his new direction. Government action had the line 'You've got to be old to get money' changed to 'You've got to be black to get money'. The group all wore Union Jack patches on their flight jackets and after only a couple of gigs, Ian had the group kitted-out in an all black, fascist style, Skinhead uniform.

Much to his annoyance, Ian soon found out that he wasn't the only one rewriting his songs, Sounds reported that a Manchester based band, The Urban Rebels, had redone Skrewdriver's terrace anthem Anti-Social, changing the chorus to 'Anti-Nazi'. Ian was not impressed.

Skrewdriver quickly became the most popular Skinhead band around, their attendances vastly outnumbering the likes of the Angelic Upstarts and The Business. There was a buzz around the group, everyone was talking about them and the music industry had still to make up its mind on how to deal with the new phenomenon.

Before the year was up Skrewdriver journeyed to Holland for a three-date tour organised by Last Resort boss Mickey French. It was a disaster that saw the band escape a big fight at a gig by exiting out of a toilet window. The organisation was an absolute shambles and the band and crew were only too glad to reach the welcoming shores of the English coast.

Skrewdriver finished the year with a sell out Christmas show at the One-hundred club. If the new sound was worrying the music media, it certainly wasn't troubling the owners of the One-hundred club, who realised that when they played they brought with them the beautiful sound of cash tills doing overtime.

# Chapter Seven
# White Power! 1,2,3,4

Not long after the trip to Holland, Skrewdriver drifted away from Mickey French's Boots and Braces/Last Resort set up. Ian remained a favourite at the shop but business ties had been cut.

Practicing in a small basement studio in East London, Ian began to introduce new material, it was unlike anything he'd done before. Politically it was totally unguarded and deliberately racist. After months of 'ifs' and 'buts', no-one was in any doubt as to what Skrewdriver had become.

The new set included such titles as Tomorrow belongs to me, White Power, Smash the IRA and Soldier of Freedom.

Dogged by the music establishment from the very start, Ian finally gave up any hope of commercial success via conventional means and plumped for the underground. He viewed the band in much the same way he viewed the social conditions he lived in. His time with the National Front had convinced him that the white Briton was the best, but was being treated second class in his own country, due to Government treachery and Communist subversion. In much the same way he saw Skrewdriver unable to get media coverage, music industry backing and yet they were packing out clubs and music halls.

Just as he had turned his apolitical life into one of a fanatical activist, he would now use Skrewdriver as a vehicle to hit back at those who had stood in his way, while capitalising on the groups potential for recruiting the young to the cause.

Running the rehearsal studio in East London was Scotty. Scotty had been involved in the music scene for some time and had played for various bands in London. When he first took the booking for Skrewdriver he was a little apprehensive. Scotty and his partner had put some money together and bought some gear, it was generally inferior quality, but then when they got the booking from Skrewdriver at fifteen pounds a go, it helped them get off the ground. It was the first session they had booked.

The band met at the studio and before cracking on with the practice Ian took time to discuss a dramatic story about the gig they had in Holland where there was a big fight. Some of the band decided to show off the teeth marks in their guitars. The engineer looked a little worried, but being in such a predicament decided to continue setting up.

The engineer later told Ian that he was a bit scared of them, but the fear was off-set by their impeccable behaviour. Other groups that went in after them were far worse, leaving chewing-gum in the carpet along with fag-butts. It may seem strange but the Skinheads actually set a good precedent. That was what influenced Scotty to give them help. Most studios would have quite simply refused any further bookings.

On the live scene Skrewdriver continued to pack them in and their popularity was bringing them a lot of attention from the left-wing. One band, Infa-riot, had verbally attacked them at one of their gigs and news had got back to the Skrewdriver camp. So, on the twentieth of January Ian and co. turned up at the One Hundred club, where Infa-riot were playing, and after a few exchanges of opinion a big fight broke out. Infa-riot fled to their dressing room where they tried to barricade themselves in and ended up getting a heavy beating.

Immediately pressure was on Nada Leslie, the promoter responsible for putting Skrewdriver on at the Hundred club, to cancel any future bookings. She told Sounds magazine that she had spoken to both singers from Skrewdriver and another controversial Skinhead group Combat 84 about the problem.

"I've told them both - nobody wants you, but I'm giving you a chance. I don't want any preaching. All the kids want is music and that's what you must give them." The paper also reported that Ian Stuart had been seen regularly wearing National Front regalia.

Had Skrewdriver been failing to attract an audience it was obvious that Ms Leslie would have dropped them like a hot potato, but while they were coming in their droves, she would hold on as long as she could.

The NF were keen to re-launch Rock against Communism and so set about arranging a concert in Stratford, East London. On the second of April Nineteen eighty-three over six hundred people turned up to see Skrewdriver supported by The Ovaltinees and Peter and the Wolf. The gig had been advertised on a word of mouth basis, a method that would become commonplace with future Skrewdriver gigs.

Dressed in black Ben Sherman and stay-pressed with red braces and a Union Jack flag worn as a cape, Ian kicked the evening off with a diatribe against the IRA and the 'traitors in government'. Between songs his mini speeches against the CND, the left and Immigration received rapturous applause and frantic choruses of Sieg heil. In musical terms it was akin to a Neurenburg rally. The fusion of an outlawed band playing rebellious tunes, with Nazi overtones, was at its most potent and the audience was lapping it up. The atmosphere was electric and if the Skinheads present needed any psyching up then Ian was the man to deliver.

Singled out for particular attention was Sounds features editor, Garry Bushell. "This one is about a bloke who's tried to stop us." Ian announced from the stage. "Garry Bushell is a cunt. This one's called I don't like you."

The Front were pleased with the outcome and quickly declared Skrewdriver as the champions of this new musical revolution. "At last there is a band with guts" screamed the editorial of Bulldog, the paper of the Young National Front.

> # BULLDOG
> MAY 1983  ISSUE No. 33
> 50 Pawsons Road, Croydon, Surrey CR0 2QF.
> Editor: Captain Truth
>
> ## EDITORIAL
> ## At last—there is a band with guts!
>
> THE MIDDLE two pages of this issue of *Bulldog* make up a Rock Against Communism special. The reason for our decision to extend the RAC News feature by an extra page is that at last a band have come along with the courage of their convictions.
>
> In the past, bands have supported the National Front at first, but have sold out as soon as they got recognition. The fact is that the music business is dominated by middle-class trendies and rich capitalists who support multi-racialism. It therefore takes a band with real guts to stand up for the White working class in such a hostile environment.
>
> Skrewdriver are such a band – we salute their courage.

"It takes a band with real guts to stand up for the white working class in such a hostile environment. Skrewdriver are such a band - we salute their courage." These were the words of Joe Pearce writing under the pen name of 'Captain Truth'.

Pearce spent time in jail for his part in the production of an earlier issue of Bulldog, the Department of public prosecution had deemed illegal. He now found it essential to relinquish his name from any official connection with the paper.

Bulldog soon became the only place to get news on Skrewdriver and the now flourishing RAC scene. Attacking Garry Bushell, it claimed that he had blacklisted the band from getting any coverage in Sounds and had also threatened any record shop willing to stock Skrewdriver records that they would no longer be able to advertise in the paper.

Bulldog made him Blacklist number sixty-eight. "Bushell doesn't give white youths the right to reply to the lies he prints in Sounds." They said. "So now we can reply to his lies personally." There followed Bushell's Kidbrooke address.

Telling Bulldog of his reasons for publicly coming out in support of the Front Ian said "I know quite a lot of bands who are members of the National Front or other Nationalist organisations. They just daren't admit it. That would be it. They just wouldn't get any more press. I mean it's a Marxist media, the music press."

"We gave them an excuse to slag us off by being patriotic. It doesn't bother us though, we still get the biggest following of all the Skinhead bands."

"They called our audience 'morons'. In the end I got fed up with it. I couldn't see anything wrong with being a Nationalist, it was natural to me, that's when we thought we might as well go the whole way."

# SKREWDRIVER LEAD THE WHITE BACKLASH

NEARLY FIVE HUNDRED people turned up to see Skrewdriver and two other bands play a concert for Rock Against Communism last month.

The concert was held at Stratford in East London and the number of people who turned up exceeded all expectations.

The first band to play were a group called Peter And The Wolves. They played a fast and furious set which went down well with the crowd.

The Ovalteenies were next on and they really got the crowd going. They have a hard core following of White racists who even hired a coach to get them to the concert. Mick, the lead singer, finished the band's set by stripping off his Ovalteenies t-shirt to show off the 'White Power' t-shirt he was wearing under it.

By the time Skrewdriver came on the crowd were really warmed up. They opened their set with the last single *Back With A Bang*, and continued with a string of old favourites including *Anti-Social* and *Boots And Braces* from the *United Skins* E.P.

But it was the newer, more political numbers which seemed to go down best with the crowd. *Shove The Dove*, *Tomorrow Belongs To Me*, *Voice Of Britain*, *Smash The IRA* and the next single, *White Power*, all guaranteed that any Black-lovers in the audience had a heart attack!

All in all it was a very successful and enjoyable evening and hopefully it will be only the first of many RAC gigs to take place in the future.

## BE THERE!

The next Rock Against Communism concert will be held very soon. Anybody who wants to see Skrewdriver and other patriotic bands live should write to *Bulldog* and we will

**ROCK AGAINST COMMUNISM — APRIL 1983**
*SKREWDRIVER*

*THE OVALTEENIES*

Joining the band at one of their regular Tuesday night rehearsals was the NF's Joe Pearce and Patrick Harrington. They had come down to discuss the possibility of recording a single for the Front.

The NF were totally inexperienced in the business of recording music and were going to need all the help they could get. Scotty was also fairly new to recording but was prepared to give it a go, and so went about hiring the relevant equipment.

Scotty set up a four-track studio and recording commenced. The over all mix was less than ideal, but the power of the songs' sentiments was bound to make it a success in its targeted market.

Although he later recorded musically superior compositions, it remained a popular song for Ian and became a hallmark for all Nationalist music to come.

It was the big bang, as Ian recalled. "The lyrics, for me, apart from Tomorrow belongs to me, mean more to me than any other song we've done. It's such a stark statement. It's there. It's very direct."

*I stand and watch my country, going down the drain,*
*We are all at fault now, we are all to blame,*
*We're letting them take over, we just let them come,*
*Once we had an Empire, but now we've got a slum,*

*White Power, for England,*
*White Power, today,*
*White Power, for Britain, before it gets too late,*

*We've seen a lot of riots, we just sit and scoff,*
*We've seen a lot of muggings, and the Judges let 'em off,*
*We've got to do something, try and stop the rot,*
*And the traitors that have used us, they should all be shot,*

*Are we gonna sit and let them come?*
*Have they got the White man on the run?*
*Multi-racial society is a mess,*
*We're not gonna take much more of this.*

*If we don't win our battle, and all things don't go well,*
*It's apocalypse for Britain, and we'll see you all in Hell.*

Within a matter of months Ian had taken the NF into new waters and was receiving a great deal of compliments from the upper realms of the party. The Front had been on decline since the Tories had snatched away any chance of electoral success in the Nineteen seventy-nine elections, by promising the electorate to take a strong stance on immigration. The new support the party was now receiving was directly linked to the success of Skrewdriver and the RAC scene.

White Noise records was setup by Joe Pearce and Patrick Harrington and got off to a good start with the release of White Power.

The White Power EP was the most direct use of politics in music ever known. With a white fist on a black background its cover was visually striking, and at one pound a copy it was soon selling like hot cakes. The single was re-pressed three times within the first few months of its release.

For Scotty it was something to be proud of, his first musical production. Only a few years later he told a London magazine the problems it caused. "I was really happy with it, it was my first single. I stuck it on the wall in a black frame and I remember friends coming in and not liking it at all. I didn't really appreciate that, I didn't really think about whether it was offensive."

As with most people in music, Scotty's first production was something he was proud of. His involvement began as a purely financial venture, but as time went on he grew a liking for Ian Stuart, drawn in by what he saw as a charismatic and a very happening kind of person.

If Scotty had not considered the record offensive then that certainly couldn't be said for Gavin Martin, who in his NME review said that White Power was "the ugliest and most evil deployment of youth music I've ever come across." The news blackout had been broken. "It's frightening to think how many are going to buy this record, frightening too to think how many are going to ignore it and the implications it carries."

The press had been given a thousand volt charged shock. The band they thought they'd sidelined or killed off, had come back and delivered a fatal blow in the form of White Power.

> I am writing to you to congratulate you on the review of the Skrewdriver single by Gavin Martin. I am glad someone has had the courage to uncover these Nazis and their bigoted rantings. I am not a believer in the idea that if we ignore the Nazis they will go away. This is obviously not true because Skrewdriver have been around for quite a long time spreading racial hatred.
>
> I myself was pulled aside and handed a nasty little bit of paper advertising this record, whilst walking past Liverpool Street Station last Sunday. I resisted the temptation to throw it away and enclosed the crap in my letter to you. I hope you will show up these Nazis for what they are and use your influence to get other papers to uncover what seems to be a Nazi foothold in the music scene.
> An Anti-Racist, Kings Cross, London WC1.
> I think you just have. — PH

# Chapter Eight
# Voice of Britain

With the easier days of the One Hundred club behind them, Skrewdriver had to adapt to the new challenges. All gigs would have to be advertised by word of mouth. One venue that was holding out on the pressure to ban Skrewdriver was Skunks. Situated at The Blue Coat Boy pub in Islington, it was an ideal venue for the RAC groups, being just a couple of hundred yards from the Agricultural pub. 'The Aggy', as it became known, was a popular Nationalist watering hole, and had welcomed a Skinhead clientele through its doors for some time. Islington was a strange place then, there was a lot of National Front activity in the area, but it still remained a left-wing stronghold.

Both landlords had withstood the demands to oust their controversial customers, not out of any loyalty to the Skins, but as a simple economic fact. The Aggy made more money in one night than the rest of the pubs in the area put together. The Police tried relentlessly to change the landlords mind. At weekends, three or four Police vans would line up outside and, at exactly eleven o'clock, would storm in and eject everyone.

Despite the notorious reputation the pubs had, there was very little trouble on their premises, the Skins realising that one false move would result in their ejection. One notable exception was when a local pub, The Pied Bull, began hosting left-wing and Gay events. The Pied Bull was a stones throw away from The Aggy, but that night it wasn't just stones that were thrown, a push bike, bottles and beer glasses rained in on the pub. The police, who were never far away from The Aggy, moved in and arrested sixty-four people - almost all of them Skinheads.

On one occasion after a skin-full at The Aggy, Ian and a few mates decided to remove the red flag that was flying proudly from Islington Town Hall. After various drunken attempts they were successful and the flag was ceremoniously burned at Skrewdriver's next concert.

Joining Skrewdriver at Skunks were Combat 84, The Ovaltinees and Brutal Attack, the latter had performed racist songs as a Punk band in Nineteen eighty-one, and had transformed their image to one of a Skinhead band and remained a major force on the RAC scene for some time to come.

Christmas time was taken very seriously on the RAC circuit and a notable event on the calender was Skrewdriver's infamous 'White Christmas' gigs. These concerts always drew a large crowd and ended in true Skrewdriver fashion with a rendition of Bing Crosby's 'I'm dreaming of a White Christmas'. The pun wasn't lost on the audience and added to the festive mood that these shows evoked.

Sounds features editor, Gary Bushell, became very vocal with his condemnation of anyone who was still prepared to book Skrewdriver, personally threatening them with a blackout of all their future Sounds advertising. For a long while he was Skinhead enemy number one. As well as slagging Skrewdriver, he began to heavily promote left causes as diverse and sinister as Red Action who had strong links with the IRA and INLA. He took particular interest in an increasingly vocal Anti-racist Skinhead-style sect that had recently sprung up. Known as 'Sussed Skins', they professed to be the epitome of the original Skinhead ideal from the sixties, pressed suits and braces. In reality they were an odd bag of two-tone rude boys, pseudo-punks and mods. Infatuated with Stanley Kubrick's Clockwork Orange film, they dressed in industrial clothes and jeans with big turn-ups. Big turn-ups being a massive fashion crime among the London Skinhead fraternity.

Skunks later lost its entertainment licence after objections from the police, including one from Commander Davis of Scotland Yard. The club would close, but not before it had crammed in over five hundred punters to see Skrewdriver, The Ovaltinees and Peter and the Wolf perform.

Skrewdriver had by now added many more Nationalist songs to their set and from an earlier demo tape, they chose the material for the next White Noise release. The tape included the songs Nigger, Nigger, Midnight train (a song about their Dutch tour) and the White Power tracks.

Ian decided on Voice of Britain. It was a bouncy tune with lyrics in much the same vein as White Power. There were two versions of the song, one included sympathetic references to the Third Reich.

*Now we have a go at the outlaw state of Israel,*
*And all the Jewish Zionists that like to keep us quiet,*
*Start a war with Germany, and gave away our Empire,*
*Remember Adolf Hitler, remember Crystal night,*

With the band now directly linked to the NF it was decided that references to 'Crystal night', the evening Jewish businesses were attacked in Nineteen thirties Germany, would have to be altered. The result saved the Front from any electoral embarrassment.

*Now we have a go at the TV and the Papers,*
*And all the media Zionists who'd like to keep us quiet,*
*They try to bleed our country, they're the leeches of the nation,*
*But we won't give up quickly, we're going to stand and fight.*

Sick Society, the B side of the single, was dedicated to Albert Mariner, an NF pensioner who, after attending a May election meeting in Tottenham, North London, died in suspicious circumstances.

The meeting, held in multi-racial Tottenham, was hosted by NF leader Martin Webster, and had ended in a riot between the NF and a group comprising of local Black youths and left-wing campaigners. Mr Mariner had a brick thrown at his head and after receiving some attention for the wound at hospital, was allowed to return home, only to pass away the following morning. The NF were up in arms because the coroner refused to issue a verdict of murder and the police refused them the right to a public enquiry.

The NF circulated news briefings to all major Newspapers and agencies, but all refused to print any mention of Albert Mariners death. The Front claimed it was a cover up to appease race relations, promptly citing the public enquiries set up after the deaths of anti-NF demonstrators Kevin Gately in Nineteen seventy-four and Blair Peach in Nineteen seventy-nine.

The campaign to secure a public enquiry failed to achieve its aims, but did however, manage to draw people from all the major right-wing parties and collectively march through the streets of London under one banner. A far greater achievement than many people realise.

Voice of Britain was met with full Skinhead approval. A left-wing fanzine had even felt moved enough by the music to praise it. The Skinheads around were witnessing something new, a scene at the cutting edge. Those among their ranks that truly believed the philosophy being pumped out into the night were in seventh heaven. Those who just went along for the ride would get off on the rebellion of being caught up in something that had 'FORBIDDEN FRUIT' stamped all the way through it.

The knocks and blows that Ian had endured in his early days with Skrewdriver, had held him in good stead for dealing with the relentless pressure he now found himself forced to deal with. They were the untouchables, the underclass of Rock'n'roll. This was not what freedom of expression was supposed to be for. The left-wing and liberals were having a hard time playing the censorship card. This was young, raw, street rock n roll, there was no capitalist backing and most of all it was out of their control. It could not be confined. Try as they did, it would not go away. Every venue in London was contacted and warned of the consequences of putting on Skrewdriver. The RAC bands would be starved of all oxygen in the music press. Normally this was enough to have any band either quit or tow the line, but this was Skrewdriver.

Ian's opponents used all the influence they had to destabilise him. Towards the end of Nineteen eighty-three a local campaign was started in an attempt to rid the area of Ian Stuart and his followers. The nearby Lesbian centre had set up a number of meetings to discuss the problem, the Skinheads regarded them as something of a joke. The Lesbians regarded the Skinheads as a serious threat. Whipped up into a frenzy of their own paranoia, they had their centre kitted out with heavy security doors and metal shutters. On one occasion they broke from a meeting to find that someone had padlocked them in. Arriving on the scene, the fire brigade were told not to help. The thought of men helping these liberated women out of a spot of bother was just too much for them.

The council looked at ways they could evict Ian. Eventually Ferndale Hotel owner, Maurice Castles, made arrangements for Ian to move out. The council and their friends in the various campaign groups thought they'd won the day, only to be dismayed at the sight of Ian and a handful of his friends setting up home directly opposite the Ferndale Hotel, in bedsit accommodation.

Ian kept himself busy. In between gigs and practice sessions, his work as National Front organiser for the Central London branch increased, receiving Branch recruitment cup from Chairman Andrew Brons. Many in the Front saw the Skinheads he brought with him as young cannon fodder, others thought they brought down the image of the party. Very few showed them any respect, after all it was these young men and women who were out on the streets taking blows and collecting fines and jail terms in the name of their cause. While they were raking in the money, the Front were happy to have their cake and eat it.

After a fracas at the North London Polytechnic between demonstrators and NF member Pat Harrington, it was decided that the Front would start an Instant response unit. It would be Ian's responsibility to gather recruits willing to go into street action with less than an hours notice. Most of the IRU was made up of Skinheads that hung around the Kings Cross area where Ian was resident, most were unemployed and so ready at hand whenever the need would arise. The situation at the North London college intensified further, when Mr Harrington was refused entry into the building by demonstrators. Ian and his crew turned up, and were it not for the presence of the police, there would surely have been a battle of sorts. The rival sections were separated and the story was splashed across the papers. Ian being described as Harringtons 'bodyguard'.

At a high profile National Front meeting, Ian, now a member of the National Directorate, stood up to report on the success of the Instant response unit and to talk about the much publicised North London Poly fracas. Getting straight to the point he said "When Patrick Harrington has finished his course , we will go down there and annihilate that filth." He

received a rapturous applause, although some of the leadership, who viewed him as nothing more than a rabble rouser, were sure to be a little embarrassed at his outburst. They also recognised that without the support that Ian brought with him, the Front would be far more marginal, saying nothing of the eagerly received revenue Ian attracted.

It wasn't long before Andrew Brons, then Chairman of the NF, resigned. The reason he gave for stepping down was family problems, but many suspected that he was unhappy with the way the Front was going. The party had been riddled with splits and coups, none more so than around this time in its history.

Back at the NF HQ in Croydon it was decided that some of the other bands from the RAC scene should be given more exposure. The Ovaltinees had self-financed there own release - the British Justice ep. An out and out National Socialist band, they travelled with a group of fanatical supporters mainly from the British Movement. At their earlier gigs they had played with the likes of the Toy Dolls and Splodgenessabounds. They took pleasure in wiping the floor with anyone who dared to question their stance. Brutal Attack had been the other band who had shone out from the crowd. Based in Mitcham, near Croydon, they were the ideal candidates for the next White Noise release. Brutal Attack were joined on the 'This is White Noise' ep by Suffolk's ABH, London band The Die Hards and Skrewdriver who provided one of the most racist tracks ever put down on tape. Originally titled 'Nigger, Nigger', this gig favourite was retitled 'When the boat comes in'. Brutal Attack's track, Return of St. George, really brought them to the fore and set them up nicely for a string of headline gigs in and around London.

# Chapter Nine
# All Hail the New Dawn

Into Nineteen eighty-four and Skrewdriver had to go through a drastic line-up change. Due to their unique position at the top of the Skinhead hit parade, there was an endless list of potential band recruits. Ian held auditions and finally signed up Murray Holmes for bass guitar duties. Murray had previously played with Aussie punk band Quick and the dead who'd produced such ditties as 'Sieg heil we're back again'. Coming in on Guitar was another Australian by the name of Adam Douglas who Ian had met at the Last Resort shop. Ian filled his last vacancy by persuading Scotty, who'd worked on Skrewdriver's last three singles, to pick up the sticks. Ian knew he didn't quite fit the image of the band but would more than make up for it with his musicianship. Scotty probably knew that if he didn't help out with the drumming, then they probably wouldn't use the studio.

The Front were looking for someone to come in and back White Noise records. They were reluctant to invest in the bands and saw the scene solely as a way to earn them a fast buck. Eventually they struck a deal with Rock-o-rama, a German outfit who'd produced various low-key punk records. The Front would accumulate the material for a compilation LP and get their cut from the pressing. Officially it would be a Rock-o-rama release. At the same time they signed up Skrewdriver for an album and single deal.

Ian had more than enough material for an LP and so went straight into the studio. All the songs they'd played live were put down on tape and Ian chose fourteen for the Hail the New Dawn LP, two for the White Noise/ Rock-o-rama compilation LP and two for the Invasion single. Undoubtedly the most outstanding track of all was Free my Land. The rough edges had been smoothed down, gone, at least for this track, was the frantic pace of punk - replaced by a more calculated and confident rock ballad. A working man's Dire Straights. It was music to the ears of its intended market. Dogged by an unfair 'hard core' tag, Skrewdriver had risen to deliver another dimension to their appeal. The title track, Hail the new dawn, is a direct English translation of the words to the German Nazi marching song Horst Wessel. A rock version of Tomorrow belongs to me, taken from the film Cabaret, also featured on the long play, along with various original compositions that Ian had penned. Track seven, If there's a riot, drew its inspiration from a Nineteen seventy-seven concert that ended in chaos and almost finished off the group.

With the album finished, Ian was now faced with the task of arranging the artwork. The back cover was simply a photograph of the group all dressed in black. His first idea for the front cover was to have a photo of the Lewisham riot. There was a particular picture showing the NF battling supporters of the Anti-Nazi League, with smoke bombs and police in there for good measure. In the end he settled for some artwork from Nicky Crane, who, as well as being chief of Skrewdriver Security, was also a dab hand with a pencil and brush. Crane's artwork depicted a Viking shore raid, a theme that RAC used consistently to the point of obsession.

The rivalry between Skrewdriver and self proclaimed 'kings of the left' the Redskins had been boiling over for some time. Previously known as No Swastikas, the Redskins had now taken to dressing up as Skinheads and making all kinds of provocative remarks in the music press. "We're on the top of the Skinheads hit list. But we won't shy away from trouble" said Nick Redskin to Sounds magazine. The bands frontman Chris Dean, whose real name is Chris Moore, worked for the New Musical Express, sister paper to Melody Maker. It wasn't hard to see why, for a short while, they became the darlings of the music

press.

Talk of trashing a Redskins gig had been going around the various Skinhead hang-outs for a while, but when it was announced that the British Movement were going to attack an open air festival where the Redskins were playing, many stood up and took note. Before long the Combat 84 crew wanted a piece of the action, as did the Last Resort Skinheads lead by Nicky Crane. On the day the BM Skins, led by 'Mick Mac' McAndrews, a Movement activist and Skinhead DJ, met up with the Combat 84 crew and wreaked havoc upon the Redskins stage, and all who dared to challenge them. With thousands watching, the Skinheads attacked the band with bottles, boots and fists, putting two in hospital. The skinhead battle cry of Sieg Heil rang out around Jubilee Gardens, on the south bank of the Thames, directly opposite the House of Commons. They then turned on the crowd, who panicked and ran trampling over each other to get away from the fracas. In the meantime the other group of Skinheads, who had earlier assembled at the Last Resort shop, made their mark on the other main stage that was hosting, Country group, The Hank Wangford band.

Daily newspaper reports showed Nicky Crane and co. on the Wangford stage wading around with cider bottles in hand. One London paper ran the story of the smashing of the Redskins and featured a picture of Skrewdriver guitarist Adam Douglas wrecking the stage props. Much to the amusement of the Skinheads, Hank Wangford appeared on a radio phone-in show explaining how scared he was and how they were taken by complete surprise. Sunday June tenth Nineteen eighty-four was a day that would forever be remembered in the halls of Skinhead legend.

Ian had been keen to hold an outdoor festival, the logistics meant that it was far more difficult for his opponents to cancel and any counter-demonstration would be lost in the countryside and deemed as ineffective. His wish was granted when, in the summer, the National Front set up the first of four annual open air festivals. These were held at Nick Griffins' fathers' farm in Huntingfield, Suffolk. An all ticket affair, it had the Front rubbing their hands in glee at the prospect of a mighty pay day. For Ian the money was always secondary, any doubt he had about the sincerity of those who called the shots were superseded by the fact that he was 'doing it for the cause'. It was this mentality that often left him open to abuse of a financial nature. Skrewdriver were joined on the day by Brutal Attack, Public Enemy, Indecent Exposure and the Die-Hards. All went down well, but Skrewdriver's finale of Free my Land showed just why they were always going to be the leaders in their field.

Shortly after the festival, Ian produced the White Noise fanzine, a prelude to the magazine and organisation of the same name that would be launched eighteen months later.

On its release, Hail the new dawn was a stunning success. You could not buy it from record stores, but the Front were finding themselves sold out of them just as soon as they'd re-stocked. The music press ignored it, but the growing number of Skinzines hailed it as an absolute must buy. The NF journal Nationalism Today said in its review "It is the idealistic dreams and aspirations of Skrewdriver that makes the band hated by the rock music

establishment". They go on to state "Ian Stuart won't be accredited with the acclaim he deserves for writing such a song (Free my Land), his politics preclude such accolade".

Back in Blackpool the local paper gave the LP a small mention, including the address of a local outlet selling it.

Hot on the heels of the release of Hail the new dawn was the RAC compilation album, No Surrender. Featuring about a dozen bands, some musically good, some not so good, it was an early indication of the flood of releases in the coming years. Indecent Exposure, Public Enemy and Brutal Attack all secured album deals with Rock-o-rama.

Financially the NF made a big mistake handing over total control to an outside label that could reap the rewards. Their short termism, and lack of belief in the talent amassed in front of them, would always be there to bite them when some groups eventually made it big on the scene. All royalties for the No Surrender compilation were being paid in records through the Front. Some groups complained about receiving nothing more than a single copy, only to be told that all the proceeds were to go to the NF.

Murray Holmes was growing homesick and so off he went back to Australia, only to be replaced by Steve Roda, a Skinhead from Bologna, Italy. Adam Douglas also later disappeared off to join the French Foreign legion, where he stayed for many years, acquiring the position of a top-ranking Officer. Drafted in to help boost the live sound was, former Four Skins guitarist, Paul Swain.

Although he liked Paul Swain and some of the others, Scotty showed a little uneasiness at the constant changes. Influencing the musical direction of the band was a tough task, but one that was made more difficult by the constant changes. Ian could have commanded far greater musicianship had he known it, but nobody knew it, apart from perhaps the people abroad, for them he was an icon. For the people who knew him, he wasn't like that. He was just like one of the boys.

Ian continued to write new material and gig in and around the London area. At one gig in a Hells Angels club in Notting hill, he was asked to play a benefit gig for an 'Angel' that had died in Police custody. The Angel in question was Black. "I'm not playing for no Nigger" was Ian's response, the atmosphere turned nasty, but some quick talking from an ex-Skinhead, who'd become close with the  Windsor chapter of the Hells Angels, managed to smooth things over.

# Chapter Ten
# Behind the Bars

*They'll try and break your spirit, they'll try and grind you down,*
*If you stand up for your country, they don't want you around,*
*You wonder what you're doing here and is it all worth while,*
*They'll never crush the pride that's in your heart.*

With their debut on Rock-o-rama a roaring success the label again requested that the band prepare for further recordings. Again Ian had enough material for an album, and so immediately got to work in the studio. While engineering and producing the songs, Scotty took a closer interest in the compositions, pushing the group in a direction that would improve the overall professionalism and slickness of their sound. The pace of the new recordings had become slower, enhancing the melodies and allowing Ian's vocals to dominate in a totally balanced way. Ian was extremely pleased with the outcome, although any move too far away from their traditional Skinhead sound would have to be calculated in a way not to alienate his dedicated following.

Any fears he had would be quickly laid to rest. On the release of the Blood and Honour LP a resounding thumbs up was received from Skrewdriver's established support. Ian tackled subjects as diverse as Drugs (Needle man), Soviet tyranny (Poland), Rudolf Hess's imprisonment in Spandau (Prisoner of Peace) and the hustle and bustle of daily life (One fine day). This was interspersed with a more general theme of racial pride.

It was while travelling home from the studio that Ian, some band members and crew were involved in a fracas at Kings Cross Underground station with members of a black gang. Quickly the air became thick with violence as the two sides fought it out, only to be broken up by the arrival of the Transport Police. Ian and flat mate, Des Clarke were singled out and arrested. Clarke had played a major part in organising Skrewdriver merchandising and the White Noise fanzine. Whatever the circumstances, Skinheads were always going to be the likeliest candidates for detention at any dispute. The media proclaimed that if you dress like a thug you should expect to be treated like one.

Charged with violent disorder, Ian and his co-defendant stood trial on the eleventh of December Nineteen eighty-five. The defense brought up the fact that left-wing activists had been giving out leaflets at the local college and in the general area of Kings Cross. The leaflets were defaming towards Ian and could certainly be seen as an incitement to attack him and his friends. The black youths failed to show up three days in a row. Without them there could be no case. The police, keen to see the pair behind bars, collected the black youths from their homes and delivered them to the court. The judge was unrepentant, and both Ian and Des Clarke received twelve month sentences.

On his first night in Wormwood Scrubbs prison, Ian was delighted to recognise Joe Pearce during meal time. Pearce had worked closely with Ian on various NF projects, and was held in high regard by the Skinheads. He too had found himself on the wrong end of a prison sentence. It was the second time that he'd been jailed for his work with the Young National Front paper, Bulldog. It was to signal the end of the paper, eventually replaced by New Dawn. Although it continued to cover RAC news, New Dawn had lost much of Bulldog's bite.

At the time of Ian's imprisonment, the Front was entwined in a bitter struggle between rival factions, it was on a course of self-destruction and insurrection from which it would never recover.

During his first spell in jail Ian began to have doubts about the NF. They had promised to make his imprisonment high profile, but although he started receiving a massive amount of supportive mail, it was mainly due to Skinhead fanzines and sympathetic international publications that had printed his address. It was well over a month before the NF publicised an article on Ian's predicament.

Jail was a new experience for the singer, one that he would be keen not to repeat. Ian was receiving five times as much mail as his fellow cons and regular visits kept him up to date with the outside world. Books were regularly sent in, and while at 'the Scrubs' he circulated his propaganda, even to the point of lending a copy of Adolf Hitler's Mein Kampf to the Rastafarian who shared his cell. Ian's muscular build and notoriety meant that he was lucky to avoid being singled out for beatings. Being a racist in a jail made up of so many young black criminals is something very short of an easy life.

Within a few weeks Ian had been transferred to the comparatively luxurious confines of HMP Wayland in Norfolk. As prisoner L25818 he drew some relief from the fact that the inmates were predominately white. The lower classification of the prison meant Ian was allowed the use of an acoustic guitar. Again he concentrated on writing new material and answering his regular large correspondence. In a letter, dated the twenty fourth of February Nineteen eighty-six, to a Kent based fanzine, The Truth at last, he wrote "The Front put an article about our case in NF News, and there are going to be articles in Nationalism Today and New dawn, so that's not so bad after all." His doubts of NF disloyalty were for the time being dispelled. "The NF seems to be doing extremely well membership wise. This is good news because as more people come into nationalism, the more committed NS people, myself and other people, can, recruit to serve the purpose to which we are dedicated. You and I know what that purpose is, 88 - AH (Adolf Hitler)."

In late February the National Front published an article written by Ian titled 'Faith in the Struggle'. It was a sign of Ian's political maturity that he would attempt to be seen in a solely philosophical light.

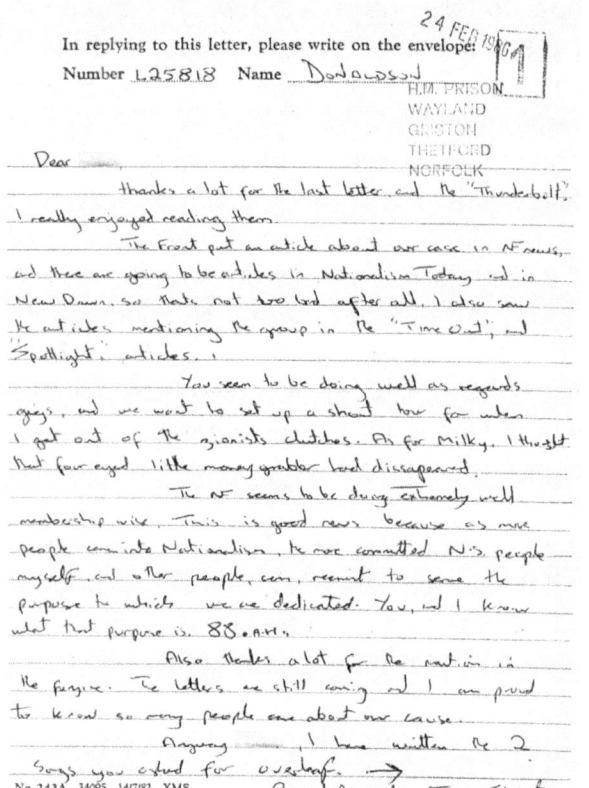

In these days of uncertainty, and political control of the western mind by the Zionist media, what have the European - and, closer to home, the British - people got to give them a glimmer of hope for the future? As you look around and see the hold that the three party dictatorship has got on Britain, you could be forgiven for sitting back and letting this tide of depression and no-hope flow over you. "Three party dictatorship ?" you may ask. It has become a three party dictatorship since the men who control the purse-strings decided that the 'Gang of four' and their Liberal allies were just chips off the same old corrupt block as the already controlled Tory and Labour parties.

Any Political party that constitutes a threat whatsoever to this monstrous set up will be viciously slandered by the puppet media, as well as being limited politically by hypocritical means (Race relations acts etc.) and finally criminalised, to attempt to draw public support away from that particular party's cause.

In a normal society the public would question why it was that their own people were being oppressed and jailed for wanting to put their own country and culture first. They would also want to know why other races and cultures were constantly promoted and feted, while their own infinitely superior history, and way of life, were severely neglected and, indeed, belittled. But this, as we know, is no ordinary society. The corridors of power, of this once great nation, have been hijacked by creatures of the worst kind. In some circumstances some of these creatures are actually British people. These traitors, even more than the aliens who control their every move, must be dealt with more severely than anybody else, when the final reckoning finally comes. These people have sold out their race and nation for personal gain.

We, as Nationalists, must overcome the most massive obstacles ever put before a political movement, before we can hope to grasp the reigns of political power. The first and most important thing we must posses is faith. Faith in the greatness of our race. Faith in the ideology of our movement, and finally faith in the inevitability of our final victory. This faith will sustain us through dark periods of oppression, captivity and even death. Faith is not something that dies with the individual, but an everlasting flame which will not be extinguished until the end of time. It is this, and this alone, which our enemies cannot destroy.

We will face increasing media slander, which we will not be allowed to reply to. We will face increased harassment by the politically-controlled police force, who, against maybe their own consciences, will nevertheless obey orders, and set us up for prison sentences that are totally unfounded. We must expect this, and be mentally and physically prepared to face up to this struggle. Only if we are ready in mind and body for the most treacherous forms of opposition will we have the strength to survive, and carry on our struggle throughout our lives. If we here in Britain are to win through to our goal, our key members, and indeed as many as possible of our total membership, must be spiritually and politically committed to our belief in race and history.

We must continue to create, and cement ties with our kindred organisations in Europe, to make sure that none of the great achievements of European culture and history are forgotten or neglected. Only by greater European co-operation can we eventually hope to offer a viable alternative to the fear-ridden Bolshevik empire, or the vulgar, drug-sodden, multiracial mess that American capitalism has become.

In the new Europe which will be created, peace would reign because of the mutual respect, for the peoples and cultures, of this once great area of world concern. No more would alien criminality, and imported vice, be rife in our cities, where a return to the old community spirit would be achieved by decent housing for all, an end to the monstrous 'tower block' existence. No longer would our rural villages and farm lands be neglected and run-down. A spirit of self-sufficiency, and pride in working on British soil for the good of Britain and the British people, could prevail. Due to a policy of armed neutrality, Europe would no longer be in an arena for U.S. and Soviet war games, and their disgusting ideologies could be kept far from Europe's shores.

To achieve all of this we, and our European comrades, must above all have faith. Our enemies are strong, and presently we are relatively weak in numbers, but unbeatable in spirit.

We must realise that we, and our enemies, are engaged in a struggle for the survival of the European races. If we fail we will be destroyed along with European civilisation; and we must accept in our hearts, that if victory is eventually ours we must deal with our enemies in the most ruthless fashion. If we do not destroy their cancer at the root we will have to face up to its reincarnation at a later stage. We must have faith in this, our battle to the death.

It was the prophecy of a Soldier about to go to war. A man who believed he had felt the bitter taste of injustice in the surrounds of a 'them and us' mentality. Here was not simply a rock star who, when the need arose, could escape to the luxury of a country mansion.

```
SIDE 1) 5          Where Has Justice Gone
                    A         D            A           D
V1   We see it on the streets today, we see it on the news.
     A            D                    B              E
     The so called British law machine, and it's us who pay the dues.
     A              D                       A
     Then we read it in the papers, that the black man gets it tough.
     A                  D             B           E
     But we all know that this is wrong, and we have had enough.
                                                    F#m
                D            A         E
CHORUS   Where has justice gone, where does it hide,
                D    "   "   "   "    A     E          A
                                    , or is it just another lie.

V2  If there's mugging on the streets today or riots in the towns.
    And we get told by a blinkered lord, discrimination brought it round.
    He says they've got no money, he says they've got no jobs.
    But neither have we, and we don't see, that it gives them the right to rob, and loo
                    CHORUS
        MIDDLE 8 = CHORUS (CHORUS)

V3  It seems we stand convicted, accused of being white,
    It seems that we are criminals, for we've not scared to fight.
    There'll be no surrender, to all our peoples foes
    We'll fight until our victory, we'll find the way to go.
                    CHORUS x 2
```

Ian Stuart believed every word he sang. His words were his life, he lived every one of those songs. It was his courage, selflessness and determination that embarrassed some of his fellow NF committee members. If they had faced up to just a tenth of what he had been through, I'm sure they would have realised that they were not the political soldiers they professed to be.

Ian chose to make his life a struggle. He rarely knew the comforts of home cooking, family life and true human companionship. Sure he had an endless stream of girlfriends and lovers, but very few meant much more to him than a one night stand. The ones he was fond of would not be allowed to distract him from his dedication to the cause. The cause had seen him attacked, shunned, spat on and jailed, but still this would not relinquish him from his goals. Of course there were many times when self-doubt would rattle him, but he kept it to himself. It was important to be seen being totally dedicated and he'd made up his mind a long time before to see it out, come what may.

# Chapter Eleven
# Media Madness

On Thursday March sixth Nineteen eighty-six Wayland Prison awoke to see a picture of prisoner L25818 adorning the front cover of the Sun newspaper. Below the headline 'ROCK STAR'S NAZI PAL' was a photo of Ian and Suggs sitting in Suggsys Mother's house. It came as a complete surprise, but unknown to Ian, someone had broken into his Kings cross bedsit and stolen the photo of Ian and Suggs from Madness. The photo had been sold on to Gary Bushell for a refuted four figure sum.

The story claimed that Suggs, whose real name is Graham McPherson, had given Ian money, helped him with his recordings and sheltered him in his north London flat. While it was true that the two had been great friends in the late seventies, the claim that Suggs had in any way helped with any of Skrewdriver's white power recordings was pure fallacy.

Suggsy may not have expected the story, but at the back of his mind he may have been dreading the day that his earlier connections with Ian would be brought to light.

Rumours had been rife for some time that someone at a major newspaper, thought to be Gary Bushell, who'd since dropped his left wing friends in the music press to become columnist with the pro-Tory Sun, was offering a reward for something that would link Suggs and Madness with the right-wing.

Suggs immediately made a statement on TV saying that his friendship with Ian had been nothing more than a 'passing acquaintance'. There was even talk of a lawsuit against News International, the publishers of the Sun.

The music press, who had no time for Bushell, who they viewed as a turncoat, supported Suggs and brushed it off as an attempt to blacken the name of Socialist music organisation Red wedge, to whom Madness had pledged their allegiance. While admitting that they had been friends in the past, the music press were not prepared to go in for the kill and the story soon blew over.

Bushell had carved away a position in the Sun as a populist writer. Here he was gunning down the defenders of political correctness, sneering at the unfashionable hippy-like attitudes purveyed by Channel four and much of televisions programmers. It was a strange game he was playing. When he championed Oi in the early eighties he was happy to turn

# ROCK STAR'S NAZI PAL

## Madness Leftie teamed up with race-hate thug

By GARRY BUSHELL

MADNESS rock star Suggsy an active supporter of Labour Party causes has a close friend who is a Nazi-style thug in jail for a vicious race attack.

a blind eye towards the strong right-wing element involved in Oi, and then when Southall exploded in his face, he was quick to rush in and promote the token Asian Skinhead or the pseudo lefty Skins as the real face of Oi. Once a member of the Socialist Workers Party, Bushell has changed sides more often than you could care to imagine. What's sure, is that he remains consistently dedicated to himself as he ever has.

Ian had an ideal opportunity to benefit from the situation, but was unprepared to use an acquaintance with someone who'd treated him well in the past for any publicity or financial gain. In an interview in White Noise magazine later that year he said "The article was just an attempt to blacken the name of Suggsy. We did used to be mates, but we haven't seen each other for a few years and that's all there is to it."

"Suggsy used to be a roadie for Skrewdriver back in the Seventies." Ian later told a fanzine. "I stayed at his mothers flat because he'd moved out and bought a house, so I had his room. I was only there for about seven months." He continued. "As far as I know we're still on good terms. He just wants to make a living. I've got nothing against the bloke."

Ian and Suggs never really fell out, but rather drifted apart. Heading in different directions, Ian soon found that an association with Madness was something he wasn't at all interested in, and Suggs undoubtedly felt the same about Ian's heightening political profile. Grinny recalled how one event prompted Ian to back off from involvement with Suggs. "Ian went to this Madness thing, I think it was for the film (Take it or leave it), he came back in no time complaining that the place was full of Jews. They remained friends but Suggsy couldn't afford to get involved as the band was getting really big then."

If anything, this episode deepened Ian's hatred for the press. The age-old practice of 'Build 'em up and knock 'em down' was still at play. Ian hated how the media manipulate people's lives as if they were just playing an insignificant board game. The media would feature heavily in Skrewdriver's choice of writing topics.

# Chapter Twelve
# Strangers to the truth

Back on the outside things were hotting up among the various NF factions. A split had occurred that was irreparable and members were quickly forced to take sides. Both factions wanted the support of Joe Pearce, who was still in jail. Ian stayed loyal to the official NF, based in Croydon, and headed by Patrick Harrington, Derek Holland also known as the 'Political soldiers'. Pearce chose the 'Flag' side, and although Ian was opposed to them, he refused to disown Pearce. Overall it was a messy business that had both sides using every dirty trick in the book.

Ian had always attempted to stay out of the divisive squabbles that eventually brought the Front to its knees. In Nineteen eighty-three the then leader, Martin Webster, had been disposed. Webster was a known homosexual, but his ability to deal with the media had served him well against those who wanted rid of him. Ian was uncomfortable about Webster's sexuality, but for the good of the party he was prepared to work under his leadership. When Webster was gone Ian continued as before, he was less interested in the party's personalities and more interested in its policies and how best to promote them. Every split in the party had dented its pride, cost thousands in court battles and withered away its membership support.

Groups such as the magazine Searchlight were particularly happy with the division that troubled groups like the National Front, and were only too pleased to play their part. Controlled by Jewish Leftist Gerry Gable, Searchlight only managed to publish about a thousand copies of their magazine. Knowing that the magazine, which solely concentrated itself with the goings-on of the various far-right groups, successfully played one personality against another, printing half-truths and rumours that often had each targeted candidate taking the bait. It was a strange situation that the magazine had such effect on those who it was set out against. Funded by donations and media work, Searchlight attempted to mould itself as the only real authority on the right-wing, a boast that often found it in conflict with various anti-racist groups, especially when it came to the often lucrative television work.

Searchlight was set up in Nineteen sixty-three by a group of politicians and journalists from the left-wing, including its then editor Reg Freeman MP. From Nineteen sixty-four to Nineteen seventy-four Searchlight ceased publishing but continued as a news agency on all things racist. May Nineteen seventy-five saw the magazine re-launched on a monthly basis and under the editorship of Maurice Ludmer. Ludmer had been a supporter of the British Communist Party, sponsoring one of its candidates on more than one occasion. Ludmer was also on the steering committee of the Anti-nazi league, a front group for the

Socialist Workers party. Working alongside Ludmer were Manny Carpel, Gerry Gable, Michael Cohen and Harry Bidney. Set up as a trust, Searchlight would be very hard to prosecute, those who tried would need generous financial backing. This left the majority of the predominately working class NF/BM supporters as an easy target for any 'outing' campaigns the group had planned. The right-wing attempted to dismiss Searchlight and also play them at their own game, the media ignored the racists claims and gave Searchlight their much sought after credence as the only true authority on the right wing.

The eighties was Searchlight's most prominent era, securing various television programmes of which they would not only star as interviewees, but would participate in the writing and directing. Their magazine was having a devastating effect on various splinter groups on the right. Individuals were targeted, their homes and work places were subject to threatening campaigns and with the might of the media behind them they were able to assert pressure on those most vulnerable to it. Another tactic was to set up a hot line, on which they would have racists phoning up and informing on fellow racists from their opposing camps.

But not all was rosy for Searchlight. Their reluctance to cover the racism that was ravaging the Middle east and being asserted from the Jewish state of Israel, saw them come into conflict with many on the left. Palestinian rights was high on the agenda of various Marxist groups. Searchlight's stance on Israel was being sighted as hypocritical. The magazine's Jewish leadership would not budge on the subject, and thus some of the respect they had come to enjoy from the left had become dented.

As the forces of the left became more revolutionary, groups such as Red action and Anti-fascist action, became dis-enchanted with Searchlight. Some of these group's practices could certainly be deemed as illegal, this, coupled with the fact that they were now treading on the toes of Searchlight, in the field of broadcasting, saw a definite split occur. Searchlight had for many years been rumoured to be working alongside the British secret service MI5, this was a compromising situation for groups such as Red action due to their links with the Irish terrorists. Searchlight was seen by some as nothing more than an extended arm of the British state, a charge that had come from the right for some years, but was now being espoused from some quarters on the left.

For Skrewdriver and Ian Stuart in particular, Searchlight would become the number one enemy. They had attacked in print Maurice Castles, the owner of Ian's hotel residence, they had launched various campaigns against venues that were prepared to host his band, they helped distribute leaflets against his presence in the area where he lived, and also demonstrations against shops that stocked his records. They had associated him with gun running, pornography and drug pushing, all of which were unsubstantiated. Ian was an easy target so they almost had licence to write whatever they wanted about him. When a proposed concert in Kingston, Surrey, was called off, Searchlight told the local press that the band due to play was Skrewdriver, who often played under the name of 'Dead Paki in the gutter'. Ian found most of these stories quite amusing, but his hatred for Gable and co.

# NAZI DEATH SQUADS' PLANS FOR BRITAIN

**SEARCHLIGHT EXPOSURE**

was real, and likewise Searchlight's hounding of him was un-relentless. While they could slander him, their attempts to fragment the RAC scene were futile. In Nineteen eighty-nine they claimed Ian was part of a 'Race war' plot to destabilise society, they cited Paul Burnley, a musician with fellow RAC band No Remorse, as a more intellectually viable option for the Nationalist bosses. It was a direct attempt to cause damage to the strongly bonded scene. The attempt fell flat on its face. Ian even dedicated a whole page in a racist music magazine to Searchlight, entitled 'Welcome to Gerry Gable's fantasy world'. The article attempted to dispel many accusations that had been aimed his way, one of which was that his band was funding the UDA.

"The Reds talk about civil liberties" Ian told the London Evening Standard. "What about my civil liberties? I can't go to a shop around here because the Communists have told the shop keepers not to serve me. The only ones who serve me are the Asians." 'That which does not destroy you, can only make you strong' is a Niezchesque slogan that Ian attempted to live by, he would not let his enemies think they'd beaten him on anything, but the strain of this was immense. Although the outside pressure was huge, it spurred him on and his response would be to amerce himself deeper and deeper into his political struggle. He was prepared to quite literally die for what he believed in. It was this dedication that amassed him an enormous world-wide support. In Britain he held the sway of thousands, he could use that to influence the support of right-wing political parties, but he never did. Nothing, not even his ego, could deter him from his dream of Nationalist power. Everything, including his personal circumstance, was secondary.

# Chapter Thirteen
# We are White Noise

What was important to Ian during the internal splits in the National Front was which group was more likely to progress and help his cause of racialist music. Pat Harrington and Derek Holland had risen to prominent positions within the Front and were willing to help Ian. White Noise would be developed into a sub-organisation controlled by the NF. As he saw it, Ian thought the Front would push White Noise with support and finance, and so he eventually gave them his full support and toed the party line towards the other splinter group, known as The Flag.

White Noise magazine was launched on Ian's release from prison. Featuring an interview with the Skrewdriver front man, giving him the opportunity to talk about his jail term and the events that led to it. Another open air festival was set up in Suffolk and so White Noise was truly launched. T-shirts, badges and records were all advertised and the money for membership was pouring in. Ian was keen to see the money put to good use, but although he was White Noise organiser, the funds were securely under the supervision of Harrington and Holland.

More bands were being formed and taking a nationalist stance. It seemed at this point that White Noise had the potential to fulfil Ian's dreams.

International attention was bigger than ever, Ian appeared in various newspapers and magazines including a four-page article in the mass distribution US newspaper Spotlight. So impressed was one organisation in the States that it wanted to honour Ian for his work in spreading 'the message'. The Church of Aryan Nations, based in Idaho, made Ian Stuart a reverend. He was unaware of this until the certificate came through the post addressed to the Reverend Ian Stuart.

The Ku Klux Klan and White Aryan Resistance were desperate to see Skrewdriver on a US tour. Representatives of WAR ventured to the UK to see Ian and his band in action at

the Summer Festival in Suffolk, and were selling videos of the show all over America.

The time spent in prison had at least served a purpose for Ian, as well as replying to the six hundred-plus letters he received, he had also written enough new material to fill at least one album. Many of the songs focused on the justice system and his experience at the hands of it.

Saturday third of January Nineteen eighty-seven kicked off the new year in true White Noise fashion. On the bill, along with Skrewdriver, were South London's No Remorse playing their first gig, Croydon's Sudden Impact and a group from Germany called Boots and Braces. The venue was a Railway working man's club in Croydon and it bore witness to a raucus performance by all, which included Brutal Attack's Ken Mclellan joining Ian on stage for a rendition of Free my land. The club was packed and the Front did a brisk trade in merchandise and ticket sales.

Croydon became an important area for Skinheads and became a focal point for a while. Pubs were easier to come by, gigs were being held regularly in the area and at least two bands were based locally.

After playing with Sudden Impact in Carshalton, Surrey, Skrewdriver drummer Scotty decided to pack it all in. He'd been thinking about it for a while and after the gig he finally told Ian his decision. He was particularly unhappy at the way people were all too often taking advantage of Ian.

At the end of the gig Scotty became involved in a row with the organiser. She was saying 'here's thirty quid each' at which Scotty's response was 'you've got to be joking.' She really took offense to it. No-one else was saying anything to her. Again Ian saw the money as secondary, many others could see that he was rich pickings for a nice few quid.

Meanwhile the Front was breaking away from its more traditional approach and embracing a more 'Strasserite' theory. There were new heroes for the NF, among them the Strasser brothers and obscure idealist Codreanu. It was indeed a reflection of the new leadership. Gone was the ultra-conservative icons of the seventies, to be replaced with the radical student-style leaders of the eighties. National revolution was the new watchword.

The previous November the Front received a new, short-lived, boost when the annual Remembrance day NF parade was threatened with cancellation. Over a thousand nationalists turned up to show their support, many were from the Skinhead fraternity, including Ian Stuart. It was a surprising show of unity, one that hadn't been seen since the Albert Mariner marches three years previous. It was bad timing for the Front who were busy restructuring and veering away from public events.

For most in the Front, this new strategy was un-inviting and was seen as a betrayal to all

they had battled for in the past. Race was no longer the central issue. The NF advertised themselves as the new champions of green issues, the environment and animal liberation.

Many of these themes would hit home with the membership, but the rank and file would always wish for the race issue to come first. It was the beginning of the end for the National Front.

Ian was not at all satisfied with the way things had gone, sure White Noise was bringing in more recruits, but the proceeds of this were being used for the Front, and not channelled back into White Noise as first promised. Skrewdriver's record sales royalties became an issue. The NF blamed Rock-o-rama, who in turn blamed the NF. Ian sent in his resignation letter. The NF leadership, seeing that they may have gone a step too far, quickly moved to quell the problem. Ian would have his royalties paid directly from Germany and the National Front would pledge more funds for White Noise. Ian, believing what he'd been told, retracted his resignation and returned to work for the Front.

It wasn't to last long, as again Ian and the Front leadership were soon at loggerheads. Ian had always been prepared to withstand the criticism he got from them. They would often pick at his writings, grammatical errors etc. Their holier than thou attitude towards their Skinhead comrade and his friends was becoming a problem. Something would have to give. Decisions would have to be made.

Ian's distrust of Harrington and Holland would inevitably mean that he would have to leave the NF and White Noise. Although he was still great friends with Joe Pearce, he was very unsure of Ian Anderson and the Flag group. The BNP and Tyndall were not likely to give him the space he needed and were not too happy with his kind of harmonies, branding almost anything not composed by Wagner as 'jungle music'. There was a feeling that he may be rendered politically homeless.

During this political uncertainty Ian was persuaded that the best way to celebrate the band's ten year anniversary was to bring out a book. Produced independently it was a fairly lacklustre affair. The book's author, Joe Pearce, spent a night at Ian's bedsit where they worked through the night getting the Skrewdriver story down on tape. Unfortunately Pearce spent far too much time waffling on about his opinion of various Skrewdriver songs and not enough space was given to the details of how the group evolved. Joe Pearce had been noted in nationalist circles for his hard-hitting propaganda. 'The First ten years' would not be remembered as his finest work.

# Chapter Fourteen
# Blood and Honour

During the Summer of Nineteen eighty-seven Ian broke away from the National Front. He never joined another party, but rather took stock of what he had. Most RAC supporters would follow him to the ends of the earth and it was this support that finally made his mind up. Something new was needed. Something that would represent the music scene and the bands. An exclusive organisation free from the confines and control of any political party. RAC fans came from all of the political groups on the right. An independent setup would strike a blow for unity, something he hadn't seen much of in his latter days with the NF.

Harrington and Holland were shaken by Ian's departure and quickly moved to secure what they could. They wrote to Skullhead's Kev Turner. The Geordie singer was languishing in a prison cell at the time, the only information he had came in letters and occasional visits.

The NF wanted to make sure that he remained loyal to White Noise. They also wrote to Ken Mclellan of Brutal Attack who had been working in the Front's head office in Croydon. They told Ken that Skrewdriver had definitely had their day and that, with the help of White Noise, Brutal Attack would become bigger than Skrewdriver could ever dream of becoming. A dirty tricks campaign was well under way. Ian's sick mother received menacing phone calls. All kinds of filth was sent to opposition targets. Ian's decision to leave had cut them deep.

Ian was more concerned with what to do for the future. He had immediate support of No Remorse who were keen to see the music scene out of the Front's grasp.

A new organisation was born, named Blood and Honour, after the inscription on the knives of Hitler's SS. It was also the title of Skrewdriver's last vinyl offering. The organisation was billed as the 'Independent voice of Rock against Communism'. The first issue of the magazine of the same name featured an interview with Ian who used the opportunity to explain the current situation on the RAC scene. Skrewdriver and No Remorse had played their first concert away from the clutches of White Noise on the fourth of June. The response at the gig was sure to prompt Ian to go it alone.

*This is Blood and Honour, a new independent rock against communism paper.*
*This paper will be run by people who really care about the nationalist music scene.*
*Not by people who are out to line their own pockets, or further their own flagging political careers, as in the case of White Noise.*

The magazine's editorial went on to claim that an account for Skrewdriver Services, Ian's merchandising outlet, had been set up in Pat Harrington's native Kensington. Any orders sent to White Noise, it alleged, would end up being cashed by Harrington without being honoured.

**This magazine will be your magazine and will be run as a service to you. We won't be pushing any one party's political message. We will mirror the views of all nationalist music fans and we hope you'll be with us in the future.**

The new magazine differed from White Noise in so much as it took on a whole new political identity. Unrestricted by party boundaries, a more radical National Socialist theme became apparent. There was a small piece in memoriam to Rudolf Hess, Hitler's deputy, who'd died, in suspicious circumstances, at Spandau prison that August. Elsewhere in the debut issue was coverage of all the major bands who'd come over to Blood and Honour. This included Brutal Attack who'd also told the NF where to go. Adverts for 'Adolf Hitler was right' T-shirts and even mention of a celebration held in honour of Elvis Presley adorned its pages. The latter was a genuine attempt to attract a wider audience. Ian was a big fan of Elvis and had his name on the membership lists of the Elvis Presley Fan club.

Blood and Honour magazine was officially launched in September at

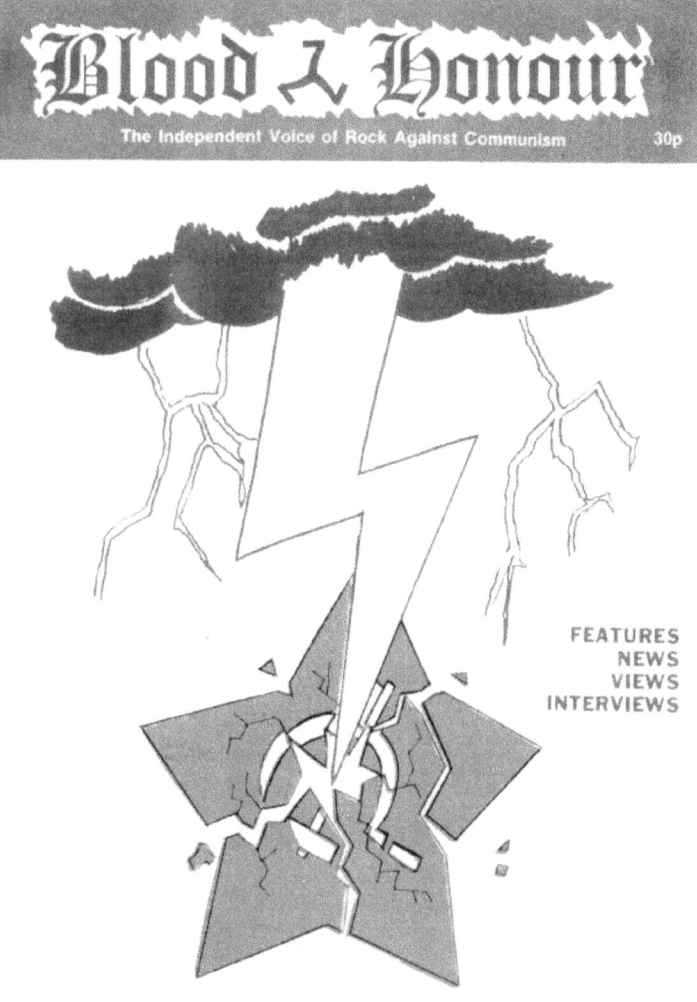

a highly successful concert that featured Skrewdriver, with new drummer Jon Burnley.

Brutal Attack, who'd been out of action for a year, returned to the scene with a whole new set. No Remorse and Sudden Impact represented a new generation of Skinhead bands. With very little promotion, and advertised by word of mouth, the concert had attracted around a thousand people. It was a sure fire sign that Ian's decision to quit White Noise was paying off.

The new air of confidence that was spreading throughout the scene had attracted the attention of the media who were queuing up to interview Ian. In the Independent newspaper Ian explained the new direction he was attempting to take the movement. "The use of music is a potent force for putting over a message. I believe we should try to do so on a European scale." With TV pictures, in August, of Skinheads gathering all over Europe to pay homage to Rudolf Hess, there was no doubting the seeds that Ian was sewing, or the fertile soil that was embracing his Euro-vision. It was at this point that Skinheads took a decidedly public turn to National Socialism.

Reporters from every major paper were eager to attend gigs. There was so much myth and lies written about the gigs that the pressmen were keen to see it for themselves. Many who did attend concerts were miffed at the professionalism displayed. Good organisation, and the fact that 'these bands can really play', took many of them by surprise. You were unlikely to encounter trouble at an RAC gig, but that's not to say it wasn't lurking underneath. If opponents of racist music had been stupid enough to turn up at the venue, the security would have found more than enough willing hands prepared to fight. This, after all, was their sacred duty. Concerts were relatively trouble free because everyone attending was of the same political persuasion and most realised that if a venue had the guts to allow them in they were due some respect. Once you'd paid the four or five pounds entrance fee, there were makeshift stalls offering everything from the latest Rock-o-rama release, to coffee mugs with Adolf Hitler's face printed on them. Blood and Honour stickers adorned the toilet walls, along with Skin gang graffiti, but the perpetrators would have to be on guard for the ever watchful eye of security. The biggest struggle of the night was getting served at the bar. The large numbers turning up often caught the landlords on the hop, and so the bar was likely to be understaffed. One consolation for finding your bar packed with bovver boys was the fact that they would always drink you dry. It was always a risk for landlords, but their was a pretty penny for those who escaped the night without trouble.

When Skrewdriver took the stage the whole world was informed. An un-nerving sound of hundreds of young men shouting Sieg Heil at the top of their voices greeted the band. Chanting often continued between songs. There was a definite feeling of rebellion and defiance. Each successful concert was hailed as a 'victory against the Reds'. Adorning the back walls of the stage was the red, white and blue of the Skinhead battle flags. Among the Union Jacks were the occasional Sunwheel or Celtic cross banners made by Skrewdriver and Brutal Attack guitarist Martin Cross. The centre piece was a huge black banner with the band's name in white. Skrewdriver's back-drop had been commissioned on Ian's return to the scene in Nineteen eighty-two, designed and made by leading members of the Essex British Movement. On stage, Ian had attained the knack of delivering a mini-speech, whipping the crowd into a frenzy and then storming straight into one of his upbeat songs. He would choose a subject, it could be a general attack on the government's immigration policy or a current news item that he could turn to his advantage. Pet hates included the CND, Garry Bushell, Ken Livingstone, Nelson Mandella and almost anyone who veered to the left. His audience was putty in his hands and, although it never really happened, he could have quite easily used this power to insight them to riot.

White Noise hardly got a mention in the press, and with their only real talent, Kev Turner, behind bars, their presence was non-existent. The move by Skrewdriver had one nothing to marginalise the scene, in fact quite the opposite was happening. Along with the media attention highlighting their success, Blood and Honour was also attracting a fair number of enemies, many alarmed at how a music scene that had been starved of publicity and respectability, was thriving right under their noses. Dr Tony Kushner, a history lecturer with

## Racists rock to a beat of hate

### by DAVID BROWNE

FASCIST rock bands, formed around a breakaway skinhead faction of the National Front, are emerging from the shadows of secret underground concerts and winning new converts to their cause of racial hatred.

A neo-Nazi musical organisation known as Blood and Honour, which already has close ties with far-Right European political parties, is also developing strong links with the Ku Klux Klan and South Africa's extreme nationalist Afrikaans Resistance Movement.

Led by Ian Stuart, who was jailed for 12 months in 1986 for a street attack on a Nigerian in the King's Cross area of London, Blood and Honour is planning to tour Holland, Belgium, France, Sweden and the United States later this year.

Stuart, aged 30, born in Poulton-le-Fylde, near Blackpool, was the NF's Central London organiser and a member of the party's directorate until he was ousted in a bitter dispute over alleged impropriety soon after his release from Wayland Prison in Norfolk.

This year, in a marked escalation of their activities, Stuart's band Skrewdriver and other groups, which boast names such as No Remorse, Brutal Attack and Sudden Impact, have played in several pubs in London, Stoke-on-Trent and other English and Scottish cities.

A Scotland Yard spokesman said yesterday: 'We are aware of this group and the fact that they attract a right-wing skinhead element. We are aware of their activities and they are being monitored.'

Speaking at his bedsit in Argyle Square, King's Cross, surrounded by pictures of Nazi luminaries and fascist memorabilia, Stuart said last week: 'Our music is for white people. If people want to call it racist then I suppose it is. We sing about pride in your race and nation, pride for fighting for what you believe in.'

Blood and Honour was in close contact with the Invisible Empire of the Ku Klux Klan and Californian extremist Tom Metzger's White Aryan Resistance, he said

'The Klan find our lyrics appealing because they concern pride in one's race, which is what they believe in. They have used our lyrics in their papers as a way of getting their message across to young people.

A squat, powerfully-built man with a Mussolini-style bonehead haircut and a taste for paramilitary clothes, he added: 'People come to our gigs because they like our music. Our songs are about things we believe in. But we are not a political party.'

A recent concert at The Star public house in London Road, West Croydon, was attended by more than 200 skinheads.

Racist insults, denouncing blacks and Jews, were hurled across the dance floor, and vendors did a brisk trade selling fascist literature, badges and records.

---

an interest in the far-right, explained. "People like Stuart are trying to start a street based European skinhead movement. There is a small fringe in Europe that identifies with the extreme right." He stressed the need not to ignore the situation. "Nationalist music of the Stuart variety has been successful in holding this together. Identification with the Nazi period can be the ultimate form of rebellion for alienated youth".

Ian spent much of his dealing with the Front who were trying all kinds of tactics to destroy his endeavour to make something of Skrewdriver and Blood and Honour. The editorial in his magazine was taken up with anti-NF diatribe. The subject of Harrington and Holland also became apparent in Ian's lyrics. One song, The new boss, drew its inspiration from the Who's 'Won't get fooled again', a song the band covered in the seventies.

We thought we had a new direction, but it's looking just the same to me,
Musical leaders, but none of them heed us, it's beginning to get to me,
Don't do this, don't do that, it's just like being back at school,
We took it all in, ignored their sins, but now we know that we've been fools,

We've been used again,
Seems like it never ends,

Although it seemed as if Ian was obsessed with his hatred for the Harrington-Holland NF, it is true to say that they were a lot more bothered about him. After all, they came out a definite second best. The Front instructed its membership that it was a party offense to read the Blood and Honour magazine. Ian had much fun ridiculing some of the White Noise boys who slagged Blood and Honour, but still wanted to read it. One fanzine editor in particular came into the firing line in Ian's 'White whispers' column. In an article, titled 'Naughty Chrissy', Ian used a mixture of sarcasm and wit to mock his White Noise enemies. Ian used the column as a way of getting back at his opponents verbally and white whispers became a very popular part of the magazine.

In an attempt to save face, the Harrington NF claimed that they were purging their ranks of Nazis. They even contacted the Board of deputies of British Jews, informing them that membership was now open to Jews. They wanted it known that the National Front had turned over a new leaf and was now committed to anti-racism. No-one bought it. Traditional racists turned away from the NF. Any fence sitters on the White Noise debate had their mind made up for them. The Anti-racists were not impressed, but saw the opportunity to widen the split in the country's foremost right-wing political party.

For Blood and Honour new ground was being made. Unrestrained by the confines installed by those who ran the NF's White Noise, Ian was finding that Skrewdriver was in greater demand. More record stores were stocking his Rock-o-rama releases and offers of gigs were coming in from all over Europe.

The group's first major venture into Europe since the disaster in Holland in Nineteen eighty two, was to the Swedish port of Gothenburg. Travelling by ferry, the trip there took over twenty-four hours. The band members used the time to get totally drunk. Once in Sweden, they were met by members of Dirlewanger, their Scandinavian equivalent. Hospitality was excellent and although there were a few hitches at the gig, the weekend was termed a great success. In Europe it was the Swedish and German scenes that were far outshining the rest, but Britain remained the innovator and most dominant force.

Soon demand was not restricting itself to Europe. Australia was witnessing a rising new Skinhead scene. It was highly unlikely that Skrewdriver would ever grace their bars and clubs, but the home-grown RAC talent was pounding out Ian's songs like the best of them. What shocked many, including the band members themselves, was that way out in the far east, the Japanese were doing a roaring trade in White power paraphernalia. They even had their own bands who were keen to emulate their British Nazi heroes. To Ian this was rather humourous. It was something of a novelty. Ian decided that they were nationalists fighting for their own land, and as long as they stayed in Japan, he saw no harm in it.

In America, Skinheads became front page news, appeared on TV chat shows and played a prominent part in the rise of the right-wing. So alarmed were the authorities that they

commissioned a report by the Anti-defamation League, a Jewish civil-rights group, to give an account on the new phenomenon. The report warned that the problem was growing. "One of the major attractions of the skinheads for young people, is their close association with a type of hard-driving rock music, called white power music." Quoting a leaflet of the Chicago based Romantic Violence group, it says the Skinheads are 'Shaved for battle'. The link between the US and British scene came, the report stated, directly from the music of Skrewdriver. Included in the report were extracts of an interview Ian had done for the Liberty lobby a while back. "I am not the type of person to creep and crawl to a bunch of weak kneed, pacifist lefties and two faced Zionists." Ian told Spotlight. "One must be honest to people about one's beliefs and especially when the survival of our race is at stake."

Organised gangs of Skinheads were popping up in all the major US cities, none more so than in Detroit where Dave Lozon became one of the areas first Skinheads. "I heard Skrewdriver, and these guys were just like me." he told the Detroit Free Press. "You're white, you've got no money. All you've got is your pride."

Skinhead involvement in the American racist groups was not always a one way street. Dave Lozon received a rapturous applause when he gave a speech at a gathering of the Aryan Nations group. Giving a run down of the Skinhead approach, he proclaimed them as the new soldiers of the right. He didn't mean the far right conservatives, but the out and out National Socialists that he aligned himself with. He finished his speech by reciting the words of a song by a British racist band.

Detroit's Deborah Kaplan, was the journalist that first alerted the area to the Skinhead phenomenon. She insisted that although there were many American imitators, Skrewdriver were still the most popular proselytizer of racism. Many US stores were selling the bands tapes by special order. "The frightening thing about the music is that even if the intended audience doesn't totally pick up on the lyrics, it certainly pumps them up." One 19 year old Skinhead interviewed in Detroit said "It makes you want to go out and hit people."

Back in England, many people shared Miss Kaplan's fears. Whenever you witness a rise on the right, you will usually see a backlash reaction from the left. This is not always out of a sudden awakening to the fear of right-wing power. It is usually out of the knowledge that they could create the latest political bandwagon, upon which their party could gain some much needed publicity and finance.

The left have found it very hard to foster their politics upon the masses in the late eighties and nineties. The use of front groups such as the Anti-Nazi league always drew large crowds.

August Nineteen eighty-five saw the launch of Anti Fascist action, a front group for the sinister Red Action. The Anti-Nazi league had been successful to some extent but Red Action had been the only real street opposition to the right wing over the past few years. With an acute knowledge of the law, they were prepared to launch violent attacks on their opponents. "The old bill don't like us." Said a spokesperson for the militant group. "They like them even less." Although they were no-match for a pub full of Skinheads, their tactics of picking off stragglers did have some effect and so their reputation was often blown up out of all proportion. Skinheads were always more likely to be arrested and so they could play on this too.

AFA had their own music set-up. Cable street beat was named after the venue of a battle between Mosley's Blackshirts and Jews, on the streets of East London. As an organisation, it was more focused on stopping White Noise and Blood and Honour, than it was in achieving success for its own bands. All the groups came from the left with the exception of their one major artist the Angelic Upstarts. The Upstarts were a popular Punk band in its post-Pistols era. What was ironic was that much of their earlier material could be found in many a racist Skinheads record collection. The group even had one single, a patriotic ballad entitled England, banned from the charts because of its nationalistic overtones. Ian Stuart often said that he wished he had written the song. The group, who had once pandered to Skinhead politics and stated that 'Enoch Powell should have been prime minister', now found themselves as the new darlings of the left.

It was a couple of years before AFA made any real impact. Once they did, their campaigns against Skrewdriver and the RAC scene were heavily backed up by sympathisers in the music industry.

# Chapter Fifteen
# False Dawns and New Horizons

Fallout from the White Noise split continued to be at the top of the agenda. Although the majority of the troops were firmly behind Ian and the new Blood and Honour organisation, the Front had managed to disrupt Skrewdriver's recording schedule. With what could well be described as nationalist music's greatest recording in the bag, Ian was eager to see his new efforts delivered to his awaiting public.

Unfortunately for Ian, Rock-o-rama had become embroiled in a financial disagreement with the White Noise club. The NF had pushed their credit to the limit and now the German label wanted paying. The Front leadership knew that if they were cut out of the loop, their lucrative merchandise business would be threatened. It was important for them to retain the support of Kev Turner, whose debut LP was also being delayed. Pat Harrington ventured to Koln to meet R-O-R boss Herbert Egoldt and pay the bill. Harrington was also after gaining political points by demanding that the record company write a letter stating that all financial dealings between the two were above board. Rock-o-rama agreed to their demands, but the letter was rendered useless as it explained that the Front had failed to settle their bill for over eleven months. It could not be used to regain some much needed credibility.

All was not lost for the Front. They could return to England with the news for Kev Turner, the new jewel in their crown, that his Skullhead LP would now go ahead without any more delay. With Kev in jail they found it much easier to manipulate him. Painting Turner as the hero and Skullhead as the best thing since sliced bread, they knew that it would take a lot to turn him. They were pleased when even their strange anti-racist turn didn't un-nerve him. The front page of National Front News showed Graham Williamson, a leading member of the party, shaking hands with a Black militant. It was indeed a million miles away from the principles the Front was founded on, and those that most had joined for.

Imagine their pleasure when Kev Turner replied to their new stance in such a positive manner. So keen to exploit the situation, they decided to publish his letter in the next edition of NF News.

> Dear NFN
> The last paper I received presented a cover that I never thought I would see. It is a good sign that our repatriation stance is being recognised by Black Separatists. I

should imagine that the 'Bigot brigade' are in a state of shock.

The last remaining strongholds for White Noise were in Skullhead's Newcastle, and in Wales, where a couple of NF fanzines were churning out the party line. Cardiff remained loyal to White Noise due to the presence of the NF group Violent Storm.

Ian was contacted by the makers of a Channel Four TV programme. They were interested in his side of the story concerning the split in the NF and the new direction it had taken. Ian went on camera to say that the Front had set up White Noise, and his understanding was that it would be used to build the nationalist music scene, not be used to line the pockets of the NF. He gave this as the reason for his departure from the Front.

The Dispatches programme was set out to discredit the Front and took much of its direction from Searchlight's Gerry Gable. In attempting to show the Front's split away from the Skinhead scene Dispatches actually showed the NF in a light that Harrington and Holland could only be happy with. Out went the Skinhead image and the street marches, in favour of student types on computers and young nationalists gathering for training seminars in the Welsh countryside.

In the centre of London, fashionable Carnaby street had fastened on to the RAC scene. They were selling T-shirts, badges and records of all the top bands, creating many of the designs with their in-house designers. The demand was immense. Blood and honour was fast becoming the latest street fashion.

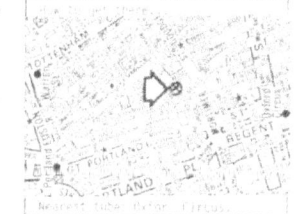

All this newly found support was not going un-noticed by the left who quickly petitioned passers-by to have the offending items removed from circulation. The shop keepers refused, the trade being too good to close its doors on. Eventually there were mass demonstrations, newspaper campaigns and even Lady Porter, leader of the Conservative Westminster council got involved.

On more than one occasion, the main shop supplying RAC goods, The Cavern, was raided by Police. They took away stocks of records and magazines, but soon found that they were forced to return them, as none warranted court action. "The shop next door is run by Indians." Said a spokesman for The Cavern. "It's not as much fun picking on Indians selling Fascist merchandise." Contrary to what the campaigners were saying, there was nothing illegal in selling Skrewdriver records and merchandise.

"At the moment they are grossly offensive and repugnant." Said a legal expert. "But they don't suggest action or use language against another racial group". The songs were direct and certainly pulled no punches. The only way they could be termed illegal, was if they actually called for the murder of someone, or threatened a specific group. Even if the records did this, the prosecutors would have to prove that the seller was aware of the exact content of the records.

When someone complained to the Jewish Chronicle, they were told that the Commission of Racial Equality, Crown prosecution service and the Board of Deputies were all powerless to stop the sale of these Nazi goods.

Taking legal action against a musician or band is extremely hard to uphold. There are so many loop-holes and pitfalls. When a record has been deemed offensive, the authorities have dealt with it best by putting pressure on distributors to drop it, thus ceasing its circulation. They had already done this to Skrewdriver and still they managed to get the records in shops.

For the left-wing demonstrators, the situation had its own dilemmas. On one hand they wanted to be seen as the purveyors of freedom of speech and expression, on the other, they were attempting to enforce a censorship that had gone much further than the authorities controls would go.

After much deliberation the Merc took out all the offending material from display. Mr Assad Salahi also agreed to stop selling Hitler T-shirts and Nazi flags, and so eventually only one shop continued selling RAC merchandise. The owner, who used the name Andrew St. John, had split from his brother Michael's business at The Cavern to set up the Cutdown shop. Unbeknown to Ian and the other bands, Mr St. John was actually a North west London Jew by the name of Andrew Benjamin. A regular at a Synagogue in Mill Hill, Benjamin was happy to mix it with the Nazis, as long as the money continued to roll in. This brought him in direct conflict with his brother and soon he found himself ostracised from the family. "We want everyone to know that we will do everything to stop him. We want to bring an end to the sale of this disgusting and offensive hate propaganda." His brother Michael was desperate to distance himself from the controversy.

The Jewish community was also up in arms. Benjamin's Grandmother awoke one morning to find pictures of herself and Adolf Hitler on posters fastened to lampposts near her Stamford Hill home. "This is absolutely killing her." Said Benjamin's brother, Michael. "She won't leave the house and cries uncontrollably all the time." The posters had been designed to bring shame on young Andrew, who later found himself summonsed to Woburn House in Central London to discuss the situation with the Board of deputies of the British Jews, an organisation whose influence far exceeded one of a small religious grouping.

While he thought about the outrage he'd cause by selling racist music, it was the constant sound of ringing cash tills that urged him on and made him spurn his advisors. As he told

# Jew sells swastikas

**By JULIAN KOSSOFF**

A Jewish businessman is cashing in on the trade in Nazi fashion, music, and literature.

In a quiet turning just north of Oxford Street, there stands a shop, with blacked-out windows, called Cutdown. Its owner is Mr Andrew Benjamin, from Hendon, north-west London, a former member of Mill Hill Synagogue.

His Jewish heritage has not stopped him from selling and exporting clothes, records and accessories that appeal to those who identify with Nazism.

Earlier this month, Anti-Fascist Action picketed the shop, believing it to be the new base for the neo-Nazi "Blood and Honour" organisation — a breakaway from the National Front's White Noise Club, with fascist links here and abroad.

Mr Benjamin plays down the significance of his business. Speaking from his shop, surrounded by T-shirts and flags with swastikas and other Nazi symbols, he said: "It pays for the car and mortgage."

His connections with the neo-Nazi music scene in this country extend far beyond the mere sale of records. Last April, a London concert of skinhead bands degenerated into fighting that spilled out into the street. A passer-by was stabbed. The promoter of that concert was a Mr Andrew St John.

"Andrew St John is an alias I sometimes use in business," Mr Benjamin told me.

In spite of last year's problems, he is helping to organise a similar concert at a secret location in May. It will feature all the top Nazi-style bands, including Skrewdriver, Brutal Attack and No Remorse.

No Remorse members are avowed British Movement supporters. One of their numbers is called "Six Million Lies."

Skrewdriver is the most notorious Nazi-style band. "Blood and Honour" is the title of one of its albums. Its lead singer, Ian Stuart, was a National Front member.

Mr Benjamin is adamant that he will continue his business. "There is nothing wrong with this. It's not illegal and people want to buy this material."

Mr Andrew Benjamin poses for the "JC" in his shop

the press "It pays for the car and the mortgage." His case was not unique. Jews in the east end of London made flags and badges for Sir Oswald Mosley's Fascists in the thirties. Another Jew by the name of Gerry Viner was often spotted selling copies of National Front News, in the predominately Jewish area of Brick lane. Benjamin was a black sheep of sorts, but he wasn't the first.

Back in Germany, Rock-o-rama was giving the go-ahead to press the new Skrewdriver LP White Rider. The display of musicianship on this album was one that musicians on the RAC scene have rarely matched since. Ian's songs were better thought out, and delivered more professionally than ever before. One thing that did let the LP down was the packaging. Many of the songs included had been written in jail and that took the theme of two of the tracks. Ian paid tribute to his heroes in the Waffen SS, and delivered a tale of their plight on the eastern front in The snow fell. A slow melodic tune with imaginatively crafted lyrics, this was Skrewdriver at their peak. I can see the fire, was Ian's favourite, this may have puzzled some due to the subtleness of its message.

*I can see the glint of belief shining in your eyes,*
*I know you won't turn back from the future as it lies,*
*You feel the anger, direct it at the people all around,*
*For it seems that they are asleep, it seems their hands are bound,*

*I can see the fire and I know that it won't die,*
*I can see the flames are burning deep inside your eyes.*

    For those on the scene who thought Ian had gone soft there was Strike force, a song that had the chant "Watch out Nigger!" edited from it before its release. Strike force was a call for support for the white racists in South Africa and had already become a favourite at gigs.

As with all Rock-o-rama's releases, White Rider was sent to lawyers to be given the all-clear. It wasn't just in England that their records had been creating a stir, there had also been demonstrations outside their Koln offices which had forced them to move premises.

Although the politics, and the methods he used to push them, never always pleased all the leaders on the nationalist circuit, there were few who would publicly criticise Ian.

Colin Jordan was one person who did speak out against Ian Stuart and the Skinhead movement. Jordan was a one time leader of the British Movement, who, after a scandal involving stolen underwear in a branch of Marks and Spencer, resigned in an attempt to cause less embarrassment to his party. In the sixties he had been a major figure on the right, mixing with the likes of John Tyndall, then in the National Socialist Movement, and currently leader of the British National party. The group made headlines by attracting the likes of the notorious American Nazi George Lincoln Rockwell to their gatherings. Since the early eighties Jordan has spent most of his time writing booklets and publishing his own newsletter, Gothic Ripples, from his home in Hogarth Hill, West Yorkshire.

One of the old school, Jordan believes in installing a National Socialist regime identical to that of the Nineteen-thirties German republic. His stand was against the modern day Western world and all it entails. Rock'n'roll music was not invented in the time when Adolf Hitler graced the earth with his presence and so was something that would be very much frowned upon.

In one issue of Gothic Ripples, Jordan claimed that "Skinheads practice the same back to the jungle method of mind bending by primitive music as those who promote the revolution of multi-racialism." He went on to compare a Skinhead concert to that of "a celebrating assembly of Central African cannibals jubilating around the cooking pot".

Ian was furious and said he felt betrayed by his fellow nationalist. Ian was one of many on the right who believed that the Marks and Spencer incident was a stitch-up. In his view, Jordan had passed his sell-by date and was living in an age that had been long since rendered obsolete. Although disappointed by Jordan's outburst, Ian laughed it off, referring to Jordan as the 'Fool on the hill'.

Jordan's views may have found some common ground in the elderly leadership of the BNP, but for fear of upsetting some of their younger members they stayed out of the fray.

The Gothic Ripples set-up was somewhat obscure and Jordan's attack had no substantial effect on Skrewdriver. The incident was nothing compared with the group's battles with the NF, Searchlight and the left.

# Chapter Sixteen
# Against Reds and Reaction

*If they'd bother to look around,*
*They'd see the writing on the wall,*
*A lot of people are waking up,*
*And answering the White man's call,*
*If they try to put us down,*
*If they don't destroy us, we'll get strong,*
*Their constant lies and harassment,*
*Only helps us to carry on.*

With Blood and Honour now firmly established, Ian was busier than ever before. Concerts were being set up on a fortnightly basis, many in the Midlands of England. In London, Skinheads flocked to various Kings Cross pubs that had become popular with RAC band members and fans alike. For Ian it was a particularly good time, more gigs than ever, money coming in from merchandise sales and a different girl each week.

With the success came some down sides. The campaign against him had intensified. There were demonstrations held outside his Argyle square dwellings. When he complained to the police on duty, Ian was told that he would have to stay in his room and if he showed his face at the demo he may be arrested.

On a couple of occasions Ian walked out of his accommodation to find a car load of anti-fascists waiting to attack him. None were successful. During one particular ambush, the assailants went away with more than they'd bargained for when Ian knocked one down, smashing out his teeth with a deadly right hook. Incidents like these only added to his notoriety. The left, who were attempting to paint him as a true descendant of the Devil, often got so carried away with their own propaganda that they ended up frightening themselves. Even the toughest Communists were wary of his reputation, a reputation that they had given him. All this brought Ian many moments of amusement.

Among the people who often dropped in on him were some Chelsea football fans whom Ian had known in their Skinhead days. One night they arrived late and after a jaunt to the burger bar in Kings Cross station, a fight broke out with some

Homosexuals who frequented the Bell pub. Fists flew and one of the Gays was stabbed. Before he knew it, Ian and three others were carted off to the police station and charged with Violent disorder.

Remanded in Wormwood scrubbs Prison, Ian couldn't believe his bad luck. Jail was a place he'd been desperately attempting to avoid, and, at a time when everything was going so well, he was worried that a break could spoil the momentum.

During the three months that Ian was on remand he stood trial five times. It was obvious that there was insufficient evidence but the authorities were be keen to keep Ian locked up. On the outside Brutal Attack continued to organise gigs, and Blood and Honour was temporarily handed over to Joe Pearce.

While in jail, Ian spent much of his time writing to comrades throughout the world, compiling lyrics and reading books. There are only so many songs you can write about prison, unless your name is Johnny Cash. Being locked away from the outside world restrains the broader influences required for those spurts of inspiration that urge song writers to put pen to paper. Ian fed his imagination with fables and books of folk tales. His favourite author J.R. Tolkein, was responsible for such masterpieces as Lord of the Rings and The Hobbit. Tolkein's books spoke of days gone by when Sorcerers made magic and powerful runic symbols held hidden powers. There was much in these stories that Ian liked to compare to his own view of how his side, the good, would do battle against his enemies, the evil. As with much successful nationalist philosophy, Ian realised the importance of simplifying things, a policy the new NF were failing to realise.

With all that time at his disposal Ian decided to try his hand at fiction. By the time he saw the light of freedom once more, Ian had finished a one hundred page novel. The story was based in the fictional land of Valaria. The Valarians were honest hard working types who faced the problem of dealing with an influx of Aliens. Many in Valaria accepted them in as a humanitarian duty and before too long the visitors were dictating how the land would be run. Eventually a band of rebels fought off the invaders and saved the day. Their insignia was a giant letter V. The novel, to be published under the title of New Dawn, was very imaginative and showed Ian in a very different light to the one he was accustomed to. For this reason Ian was reluctant to push for its publication. In many ways he was a little unsure of how it would be received. Although he was encouraged by the few people who'd read it, Ian was not too worried when it wasn't returned. Ian had given it to Nicky Crane for the purpose of illustration. A modest man, Ian was often the prophet of his own misfortune. There were not many people on the right who could have written such an creative piece of work. Many of their publications were blunt and lacking in visual appeal.

Much to the disappointment of the Searchlight representative present in the courtroom, Ian was finally freed at Islington Magistrates. The Judge said the case could not continue due to lack of evidence. On his release Ian stayed in South London for a week, just to let the heat die down.

The following weekend the People newspaper had an in-depth three-page special on the rise of Blood and Honour titled Evil face of Youth. 'Dead-end twisted yobbos' was how B&H followers were described. Journalists had been allowed to interview Skinheads and take pictures of the band at a small concert held in Stoke-on-Trent, Staffordshire earlier in the year. What annoyed Ian most about the slaggings he, his group, and his fanatical followers received in the press, was the fact that some of the journalists had seen enough not to report the usual stereotypical mis-representations.

Ian felt that even if a pressman had come to a concert and been treated to a fantastic musical exhibition, they would have still resorted to the editorial line of 'They are Nazis, so they are scum'. Of course he could not claim that all his audience were angels and that all the support groups had chart potential, but there did seem to be a definite pattern to the press reports. The media would almost always home in on the guy with the most tattoos, or the drunk mouthing obscenities. These people would be photographed and quoted as the spokesmen of the movement. What often alluded Ian and his friends was the fact that the press were not there to report on a news item, but rather to find a story. Newspaper stories without the juicy bits, no matter how factual, don't make it into newsprint. The journalists involved, however well intentioned, knew this only too well. And so the Circus continued.

Some people would say that bad press is good press, or there is no such thing as bad

press. Of course it was a measure of Ian's success that they were pounding down his door to get him in their photo-frame. Pleased with the exposure he may have been, but he certainly had no friends in print. "ON TOUR WITH BRITAIN'S SICKEST BAND." Screamed the swastika laden article. "THE NAZI LOVING GROUPS OUT TO CORRUPT OUR KIDS."

Venues were hard to come by, Landlords prepared to risk a booking were worth their weight in gold. For this reason Ian employed a strong team of bouncers, known, by the letters emblazoned on their shirts, as 'Skrewdriver Security'. They ensured that concerts passed without incident. The politics of the bands was the one thing that scared promoters off, unfortunately for them, get rid of the message and you get rid of the scene. There was also the fact that the RAC scene was very anti-drugs. Drugs did not fit in with the blood and purity theme of the movement. Anyone thinking of passing around a joint or scoring dope was in the wrong place. In Nationalist eyes drug culture equals black culture. As in most of their rules and regulations, there are no grey areas. Cross the line and you will not find yourself being politely asked to leave, but end up on the wrong end of a pair of Doctor Martens.

As with most of Skrewdriver's history, every cloud delivered some kind of silver lining. Rock-o-rama were particularly pleased with the way things were going, and so wanted to capitalise on it. The German label wanted to capture the top names on the RAC circuit and tie them to three year deals. In the early part of Summer Nineteen eighty-eight, Skrewdriver, Brutal Attack, No Remorse, Sudden Impact and Vengeance all signed deals at an evening session in the Kings Cross pubThe Prince Albert. It was good news for Blood and Honour. They would be given a constant supply of fresh releases upon which to build their movement. From that day on the vinyl flood gates opened. All five bands would be asked to record two LP's a year and Ian would also move into recording as a solo artist. It was a shrewd move by Rock-o-rama, low budget productions and a constant flow of releases in a market that they almost exclusively controlled would pay excellent dividends.

Every person that ever picked up a guitar, bashed a drum skin with a stick or mimed their favourite songs in the mirror, would jump at the chance of a recording contract, however lopsided the deal was. Interest in the scene grew, new bands sprouted up everywhere and groups who'd been happy to plod along now got their acts together. To see your work presented in Vinyl form was every budding musicians' dream. For many Skinhead bands it was a dream that they were now in reach of realising.

# Chapter Seventeen
# Nazi Chic

With the benefits of readily available recording facilities came the pressure to comply with contractual demands. Two full length recordings a year was a tall order for most. Needless to say in many cases quality control went out of the window. Without the guidance of professional producers, and on a small budget, most bands fell at the first fence. The main three, Skrewdriver, Brutal Attack and No Remorse, rose to the challenge and did better than most. All would probably agree that their recordings could have benefited by the services of a skilled producer. These bands were used to learning things the hard way but the audience were certainly not complaining.

Ian soon got to work on his next recording venture. After the Fire was the last recording that would involve producer Scotty. Rock-o-rama were not so keen to allow Scotty a large say over things. He had argued with them over contractual matters and although they realised they would not be able to rock the boat too much, where Skrewdriver were concerned, they were keen to avoid paying realistic prices. Some bands could record for a quarter of the price Scotty wanted, but in real terms he was charging next to nothing. The quality of their records had got Skrewdriver places and made them THE band on the scene. Scotty wasn't prepared to cut corners just to lessen Rock-o-rama's financial obligations.

In the end Rock-o-Rama boss, Herbert Egoldt was becoming absolutely ridiculous. The studio was asking for a couple of hundred pounds more, when It should have been asking for thousands. This spelt the end for Scotty who objected strongly to Rock-o-rama's intervention. Finding it impossible to get the money from Rock-o-rama, the studio decided to break their ties. Although disappointing Ian, it was sure to please Rock-o-rama, who hated anyone getting too close to Ian in a business sense.

As with the White Rider recordings, Scotty supplied the majority of musicians and played on all the tracks himself in one capacity or another.

In answer to some of the minor criticisms White Rider had received, Ian made a deliberate attempt to add a rougher edge to his new recording.

The theme of Ian's new album hadn't changed much from his previous offerings. Forty-six Years, a song about Rudolf Hess, almost an update on the track Prisoner of peace that featured on the Blood and Honour LP. Land of Ice was written as a tribute to the nationalists who made the band so welcome when they ventured to Sweden in Nineteen eighty-seven. The song included one line sung in Swedish. One song that did surprise a few people was Ian's rendition of a song about First world war soldiers, entitled Green fields of France. A slow ballad depicting the sad tale of the loss of life upon the battlefield, Ian sang Green fields of France with a slight hint of an Irish accent for added effect.

Track seven, Time of Change, came as no surprise to anyone. A direct attack on the leaders of the National Front, the faction he would have once defended with his last breath, but now referred to as the Nutty Fairy party.

> *Stood against us are the scum,*
> *They are worried, because our time has come,*
> *One that called himself a revolutionary, turned out to be a Gay,*
> *Mummy's little rich boy, It's a time, a time of change,*
>
> *They call themselves political soldiers,*
> *But they have a massive yellow streak,*
> *A soldier has strength, but they are bent,*
> *Limp wristed and weak,*
> *Pathetic little mummy's boys, there was nothing that they wanted for,*
> *But come the day when they have to pay,*
> *We'll see who they've been working for.*

Harrington made no secret of the fact that on occasions he had met with members of MI5, the division of the police that was responsible for keeping a check on the right wing. For those closer to the mechanics of the political world this was nothing to be worried about, the rest of the right wing viewed the situation with much suspicion. They may not have had the insight to the entire workings of the authorities, but many had been on the wrong end of police operations made possible by deals and informants. In nationalist circles the police were not to be trusted.

As well as recording After the Fire, Ian had used the same studio time to lay down two tracks for a single. Showdown, was financed jointly by Cutdown and Ian Stuart. It was a deal that Rock-o-rama viewed with discerning eyes, but aware of the delicacy required to keep their number one earner on their books, they allowed play to continue.

White Rider had delivered the cleverly crafted words and masterfully astute music of The snow fell, but the new single climbed new peaks. The sound was as professional, but the lyrics, beat and delivery had encompassed a new venom not seen in Skrewdriver since their early White Power release.

*Look to the future, Outlaw,*
*The storm is coming now, Race war,*
*The skies darken as night falls,*
*The battle's coming now your race calls,*
*Carry on the fight 'till the day we die,*
*Against the people that would kill us for the flags we fly,*
*We won't surrender, we won't give in,*
*We'll fight the fight and we will win now,*

*Stand up beside us, and we will have our day,*
*Stand up against us, get out of our way,*

*People to the left, people to the right,*
*People in the middle that, don't wanna fight,*
*Traitors fight against us, showdown,*
*People in the middle get knocked down,*
*We fight for freedom, we fight to win,*
*The colour of our uniform's the colour of our skin,*
*We've got the power, we've got the pride,*
*When we get the unity it's all right.*

Still the music press ignored Skrewdriver, only mentioning them whenever there was an anti-fascist rally or demo. Their reluctance to report on them combined with Ian's determination not to be beaten had allowed the group to acclaim a new status as the real force of rock n roll rebellion. On the working class streets of England's major towns and cities they had become the new chic. Support was not confined to the rank and file of the Skinhead movement, there were all kinds of youths travelling into central London to try and get a glimpse of the new demagogue and buy his new releases. If a long term plan could be put in place and the new phenomenon be cultivated, then Skrewdriver could surely surpass the short life span that was usually associated with the latest vogue. The aim was to become a permanent fixture of inner city culture. A culture upon which nationalist parties could use to bolster their recruitment drives.

To his vast opposition the matter would have to be resolved sooner rather than later. Campaigns and demo's had done nothing to harm the band, in fact quite the opposite, so other tactics were considered. It wasn't just left-wingers who were showing concern, Scotland Yard, decided to set up a unit to monitor Blood and Honour, after becoming alarmed at their rise. The pressure was rising.

At the beginning of Nineteen eighty-nine Skrewdriver held a concert in up-market Swiss cottage. The North Star, situated on the Finchley road, was fairly small but had an upstairs hall that had held more than its fair share of rock concerts and private functions. On his way to the concert Ian had met up with Ken Mclellan, the vocalist of Brutal Attack. The two had decided to go for a quiet drink in another local pub to discuss the nights gig and talk over various plans the two groups had for the future. While enjoying a drink, the pub doors flew open and in rushed fifteen men armed with bottles and baseball bats. Ian was hit over the head and a fight ensued. If it hadn't been for the quick thinking actions of Mclellan, Ian's wounds would have been far greater. As it was, he later received twenty-six stitches, but really they looked worse than they were and Mclellan had come off relatively unscathed.

Returning to the North Star Ian was immediately surrounded by concerned friends who

were all for scouring the area to take revenge. Ian's reply was to launch into a tirade of hatred directed at his assailants, whom he believed to be members of Red Action. This was followed by a powerful rendition of his musical racist repertoire. He refused to wipe the blood that was dripping down from his shaved head onto his 'We've got the power' T-shirt. It was as much for effect as it was a sign of defiance to those who would try to stop him. When the dust had settled Ian's violent opposition had achieved nothing but improve his standing in nationalist circles as a martyr and street warrior. All subsequent photographs of the gig were put to good use as Blood and Honour propaganda.

To National Socialists, Nineteen eighty-nine was a special year marking the one-hundredth birthday of their founding father Adolf Hitler. Celebrations were planned all over the

world. In South Africa many elderly Germans gathered to pay their respects, in America Nazis flew a sixty-foot banner from the back of an airplane proclaiming their idols centenary. In Britain the media was focused on one man - Ian Stuart. Many people in the rank and file of the BNP or NF would have loved to have made a more public display of affections for Hitler but knew that it could induce unwanted bad publicity for their party. Ian Stuart was not such a man. In a full colour photograph, taken inside his cramped living quarters in Kings Cross, Ian stood surrounded by pictures and paraphernalia depicting his love of everything White. Clutched in his hands a blood stained swastika banner. Keith Dovkants had, on behalf of the London Evening Standard, come to see 'The Man Who Loves Hitler'.

"I admire everything Hitler did, apart from one thing." Ian stated boldly, leaving Dovkants with the obvious question. "What's that then?" predictably he replied "Losing." The reporter knew that he was not talking to a crank high on warped fantasies, but a charismatic and determined leader who was quite capable of making more than just a nuisance of himself. 'There is nothing compromising about Ian Stuart' Dovkants wrote, 'He is a Nazi, a racist and according to his record, a thug. He is also at the centre of a Nazi revival that has prompted excoriation from the Left and profound unease elsewhere.'

Dovkants had also spoken to a senior member of the Jewish Board of Deputies who had named Ian the most anti-semitic man in Britain. He was quite simply public enemy number one. It was an accolade that brought a grin to his face. He had amassed a great number of enemies as well as supporters.

The Board of Deputies were extremely worried that Blood and Honour was turning London into a mecca for young Nazis. Reports on the situation were appearing in Jewish Chronicle on a weekly basis. The Jewish lobby was particularly disgusted by Andrew Benjamin's refusal to stop selling RAC goods. In one front page article 'JEW SELLS SWASTIKAS, Benjamin enraged his inquisitors. When asked how he could sell Nazi wares, and still be a Jew, he told them "It pays for the mortgage. People want to buy it."

Most of the opposition to Cutdown was coming from either left-wing or Jewish quarters, but one Black newspaper ran the story under the headline 'Shop of Horrors'. David Upshall, the news correspondent, had visited the shop and been repulsed at the sight of Hang Nelson Mandella T-shirts hanging alongside Soul Power patches. Des Clarke, who was working as shop assistant and shop security under the name of Phillip Clarke, insisted "We're not a racist shop. There is a demand and we meet it." Benjamin went further. "A lot of the Skinheads who buy White Power goods also purchase Soul and Ska records.

To a lot of them it's a fashion thing."

The National Front, of the Patrick Harrington variety, were also keen to attack Benjamin,

# THE SHOP OF HORRORS

**Trendy West End shop makes profits on race-hate T-shirts and badges**

Fascist youth culture is gaining a foothold in London's most fashionable places and causing alarm among local black people and anti-Nazi groups.

By David Upshal

At the centre of the storm is the 'Cutdown' shop, in London's West End, which sells a range of White Power, skinhead and Nazi merchandise, including Swastikas and "Hang Nelson Mandela" T-shirts.

### Complaints

The original Cutdown in trendy Carnaby Street closed down after complaints about fascist material by Westminster Council, Labour MP Jeremy Corbyn and Anti-Fascist Action (AFA).

But The Voice found a continuing brisk trade in "golliwog" badges, Nazi "death's head" insignias and replicas of the Iron Cross, Nazi Germany's highest medal of honour.

The fascist skinhead organization 'Blood and Honour', which has links with the Ku Klux Klan and South Africa's extremist AWB, is alleged to have set up base at the Green Man pub, just two doors from Cutdown.

Black nurses at nearby Middlesex Hospital have expressed such fear that their union has accused the shop of "stirring up hatred against ethnic minorities."

### Demand

And a number of students from the Central London Polytechnic who live and study in the area have also complained of race threats against them.

But shop managers, Andrew Benjamin and Phillip Clarke, insisted: "We're not a racist shop - there's a demand and we meet it. It's all to do with money and we're not interested in the politics of it."

They maintain that nothing they sell is illegal and the controversy is "incredibly unjust."

"It's not coloured people who are complaining," claimed Mr Clarke. "It's communists stirring up trouble." Both are adamant that their goods do not insight racial hatred.

"It's a real hypocritical thing if you say you're proud to be white you get in trouble," said Mr Benjamin. He added: "A lot of the skinheads who buy white power goods also purchase soul and ska records. To a lot of them it's a fashion thing."

### Fumed

However, an astonished Rajan Datar, member of ska band Maroon Town, fumed: "If any of  our records are being sold there, I'll have it stopped. Anyone with any brains should realize that ska music is about black pride."

The AFA are stepping up their campaign to get Cutdown closed and expose the growth of a fascist youth movement in Britain by picketing the shop.

"By selling these goods they are encouraging people who go out and attack others," said an AFA spokesperson.

**FASCIST FASHION:** Cutdown's offending goods

but this was for very different reasons. Knowing that an alliance between Ian Stuart and a Jew could harm his reputation, they banged on about a history of Zionist and Nazi collaboration. In their eyes Ian was putting disillusioned white youths at risk. These same youths were supposed to find refuge in the Front's new music venture, Counter culture. Much to their annoyance it didn't quite work out that way.

Benjamin was no Zionist, he was simply interested in one thing, money. Their was no hidden agenda, it was simply business.

Although a little uneasy about Benjamins' heritage, Ian felt that, as long as Blood and Honour would benefit from the situation, it somehow didn't compromise his position. The means justified the end. That said, if Benjamin had introduced himself as a fully fledged Jew, and not Mr St. John whose parents were Portuguese, then it could have been a very different story.

The constant pressure and campaigning had done nothing to deter Cutdown from enhancing their presence on the RAC scene. The previous year they had staged a massive Skinhead concert in a top central London venue. The gig had featured top Oi bands, including Skrewdriver's arch rivals The Angelic Upstarts. Trouble was predicted and trouble their was when, into only their first song, the Upstarts were attacked, a sea of right-arm salutes were accompanied by huge cries of Sieg Heil. Much to the dismay of the oi bands present, the concert was abandoned. The show was eventually featured in a European documentary in which the programme makers were quick to home in on footage of Ian Stuart standing a few yards from where the trouble had begun.

Just six months on from the 'Main Event', Cutdown was planning another. This time the headline band was Skrewdriver. Publicity went out stating that the venue would be kept secret and that it would be a ticket-only affair.

The 'Main Event II' concert was to signal the end of the relationship between Blood and Honour and Cutdown.

Benjamin had booked three halls situated around London, booking them all under the name of International Music Exchange. Looking back it was doubtful that he had ever had any intention of seeing the whole thing through, and his choice of venues would indicate that. Just two minutes from Ian Stuart's front door, in the heartland of the loony left, Benjamin hired Camden town hall.

For weeks prior to the concert, left-wing activists had tirelessly gone around to almost every venue in the capital warning them of the prospect of two thousand racist Skinheads turning up at their premises. It wasn't until the morning of the gig that all the cancellations were revealed in the national press.

Mr Benjamin wasn't too bothered, he was doing a brisk trade at his Riding House Street shop. Thousands of Skinheads had come from all over Europe and North America and, on arrival in London, headed straight for Cutdown. Meanwhile Ian and other RAC band members were scouring lists of venues in the hope of securing a very late booking. By mid-afternoon a venue had been booked. The Red Lion in Gravesend, situated near the London-Kent border, had agreed to cancel their Wedding party and allow the venue to be turned over to Blood and Honour. Not only did they receive three times their usual booking fee, it was also the best bar takings they'd ever had. A venue that normally housed around three

hundred was attempting to facilitate nearly one thousand, it wasn't long before the beer ran dry.

The sets were short but most bands managed to get on. backing Skrewdriver were Brutal Attack, No Remorse, Squadron and Skullhead who were now firmly in the Blood and Honour fold. No-one ever showed any discourse at playing second fiddle to Skrewdriver, it was viewed as something of a privilege.

Blood and Honour had grown so big that the usual pub venues were now too small to house them, but booking larger concert halls was a much tougher prospect. It was one side of the organisation's achievement that the RAC leaders had yet to successfully exploit. Had it all gone to plan Ian and co. could have easily been playing to a crowd in excess of two thousand. Many supporters had been left stranded at meeting points, got lost on their way to Kent or been chased off by mobs of anti-racists who were roaming around central London.

Soon after the Main Event, Cutdown closed down, but not before concocting a deal with Gerry Gable's Searchlight. Seeking to re-establish his links with the Jewish community, Benjamin required a letter from Searchlight stating that he had only worked with the Nazis because of fears for his own safety. He wanted to be seen as an innocent party who had only taken part because of the threats that had been made to him and his girlfriend, Jane Donovan.

Gable, thinking that he was on to some prized information, agreed to the letter. In return Benjamin gave him lists that he pertained to be members and supporters of Blood and Honour. Searchlight immediately found buyers for their exclusive. The list had included serving members of the Armed forces. What Gable didn't know was that the lists were simply those of Cutdown's mail order operation. When one Scottish newspaper printed a selection of names, it was bombarded with complaints. Many on the lists, who had been accused of being hard-core racists, had sent money to Cutdown in exchange for Soul records and Specials T-shirts. There was a lot of egg on a lot of faces. Gable and the subsequent newspapers were lucky not to be on the wrong end of law suits.

The following issue of Searchlight featured an in-depth two page spread entitled Portrait of a Collaborator. Gable didn't mince his words, calling Benjamin 'a con man, cheat, porn-broker and Nazi-lover'. He also stated that 'his vilest act was collaborating with the enemies of his people'. Searchlight delved into Benjamin's affairs to find that he'd given up selling racist merchandise and had started a mail order business that offered explicit porn videos. This new venture included Black and Asian Sex films.

# Businessman who sold Nazi regalia is jailed

**JEWISH CHRONICLE REPORTER**

A Jewish businessman who sold neo-Nazi regalia at a West End shop has been jailed for two months by Guildhall Crown Court.

Andrew Benjamin, 28, of Hampstead, North-West London, admitted behaviour likely to stir racial hatred by selling "offensive and abusive" material.

Benjamin, who was once a member of Mill Hill Synagogue, opened the shop called "Cutdown," just off Carnaby Street, in 1988, where he sold clothes and records with a neo-Nazi theme.

After protests from local residents, he moved to premises the other side of Oxford Circus.

In 1989, he organised a concert featuring top Skinhead bands, including No Remorse. One of their numbers was a Holocaust revisionist rant, entitled "Six Million Lies."

In an interview with the Jewish Chronicle in 1989, Benjamin said: "There is nothing wrong with it [neo-Nazi fashion]. People want to buy this material and it's not illegal."

For Benjamin it was simply business. As one venture closed so another appeared. The only thing that would finally defeat him was his own ego. Although visibly frightened by the mere thought of a violent encounter, he thought he could out wit them all. In the heyday of Cutdown he was eager to cram as much stuff on his shelves as possible, no matter what the quality. He was keen to sell bootleg videos and cassettes because the profit ratio was so great. One video that he had been warned not to sell was just too much of a temptation. On the third of December Nineteen ninety-one he was jailed for two months for behaviour likely to incite racial hatred. Benjamin was distraught, he always thought that jail was for other people.

# Chapter Eighteen
# Reich 'n' Roll

*"A pamphlet is read only once, but a song
is learnt by heart and repeated a thousand times"*
- Ian Stuart.

It was obvious from the lengths that the opposition would now go to, Skrewdriver would have to find new methods to operate. One such method worked out well and embarrassed the media into the bargain. No Remorse had sent out cassettes of some of their less controversial songs under the false band name Valhalla. Almost all of the clubs receiving them wrote back favourably and offered them slots on their gig circuit. On one such night, in April Nineteen eighty-nine, No Remorse were asked if they knew of another band who could accompany them in playing live. Within a few days the clubs adverts were being run in all the major music papers. Valhalla and Strike Force live at the Cave. Strike force being a

cover name for Skrewdriver. The Cave was an impressive disco in Islington and its owner was one Paul Solomon.

On these occasions the Skin bands never knew quite what to expect, the first obstacle was to ensure that they got in without too many questions. Once the bands and road crew were in it was almost impossible for the promoter to stop the proceedings. The Cave gig went well, the audience responded favourably and there was something of a party atmosphere present that night. What astonished Ian was the fact that Mr Solomon was keen to have them back. At first he assumed that he was just being sweet talked until all the Skins had safely vacated the premises. Ian was surprised when he later received a call confirming a second booking.

Unfortunately for Ian it wasn't too long before the cat was out of the bag. NME were backtracking and covering their blushes, embarrassed and bewildered at how they could have advertised a Skrewdriver gig in their pages. Islington Council were none to pleased with Mr Solomon, and threatened him with the withdrawal of his entertainments licence if he ever played host to a RAC gig again. Needless to say the second booking never materialised.

The scam had worked well and both bands had managed to secure a handful of gigs that way. At one gig at the Tunnel Club in Greenwich, South London, a fight broke out which brought an end to the use of that particular venue. Some ex-Skinheads had come along to see Skrewdriver and were upsetting a small group of Skins by throwing their weight around. The group of Casuals was led by Chubby Chris, one time singer of the band Combat 84, and Charlie Sargeant, later of Combat 18 infamy. When it went off they probably thought they were taking on ten Skinheads at most. When a large proportion of the audience and some members of the bands joined in, it caught them by surprise. Skrewdriver guitarist Ross McGarry pulled out a stun gun and promptly zapped Charlie Sargeant. The Casuals found themselves backed into a corner. Chubby Chris had to rely on some quick talking to stop them all from receiving a thorough beating. "We're all white, we ought to stick together." The Casuals were glad to get out with their lives.

Outside of the Capital, gigs were easier to come by. Skrewdriver started to appear regularly in and around the county of Nottingham. It was an area that would soon become Ian's permanent place of residence.

In response to the growing scenes in Europe, Skrewdriver found themselves headlining various concerts around the continent. Sweden was a popular haunt, as was Germany, where, at Neiheim, over a thousand German racists turned up to see their heroes on their Break the chains tour.

Concerts abroad had a very different atmosphere to those held in Britain. At home Ian knew most of his audience by sight and although they had nothing but respect for the Blood and Honour leader, their affections never really boiled over into hero worship. Abroad his fanatical supporters looked upon him as something of a God. On arriving at the venues Ian would often find a long queue forming. They were lining up to meet him, acquire his signature or generally be in his presence. Many in the world of Pop music would let their ego get the better of them, not so with Ian. Certainly touched by the massive show of affection, Ian saw it more as an opportunity to channel this appreciation towards the cause he'd championed. The situation was often harder to deal with than one would first assume. After giving his all on stage I'm sure he would have rather disappeared for a while to catch his breath, but Ian knew his responsibilities and lived up to them well. Most rock bands have hardly any contact with their supporters, other than the token hand in the audience or after show parties, with Skrewdriver it was the complete opposite. After playing their live set the band would come off stage and re-join the audience, usually in the bar area.

With Scotty now completely out of the picture, Ian would have to find a new place to record his songs. Ken Mclellan said he'd try to help and eventually Ian booked into a studio in Croydon. The studio had been used by various Blood and Honour bands, including Brutal Attack.

Des Clarke's move into the Rock-a-billy scene had a large influence on Ian's next recording venture. Rock-a-billy had attracted many young people with an aversion to multi-racialism. The scene was almost as exclusively white as that of the Skinheads. This new culture made use of the American southern states Confederate flag, a symbol, to many, of rebellion and white supremacy.

For his new project, Ian leant heavily on the influence of Elvis Presley and the songs of the Ku Klux Klan from the Sixties. Joining up with a talented seventeen year old guitarist and a competent double-bass player, both playing in one of the most popular Rock-a-billy bands of their time. With the inclusion of his Skrewdriver drummer, Ian formed The Klansmen.

The new band members assumed the stage names of Jeb Stuart, Bones, Jed Clampett and JB Forrest. It was a deliberate attempt to disguise the identities of the two Rock-a-billies. The names came from the Confederate side of the American civil war. The concept was not totally original as in the Sixties a top billing Country singer recorded various racist and pro-Klan songs under the guise of Johnny Reb. The Klansmen payed due to this fact by recording their version of Johnny Reb's 'Stand up and be counted'.

The usual Rock-o-rama restrictions prevented the band from delivering the sort of unguarded racism that Johnny Reb had produced twenty years before them. The Klansmen did manage to achieve a quality that would compare to much of the material on the Rock-a-billy scene. The only song on the album that bore any kind of resemblance to Skrewdriver was a cover of Chuck Berry's Johnny B. Goode. Re-written and re-titled Johnny joined the Klan, it received Skinhead acclaim at Skrewdriver concerts.

*Way down in Louisiana, across to New Orleans,*
*Way back up in the woods, down by the Evergreens,*
*There was an old cabin made of earth and wood,*
*There lived a country boy named Johnny B. Goode,*
*Didn't like muggers taking over his land,*
*Johnny got clever joined the Ku Klux Klan,*

The general suppression of Ian Stuart's music meant that he could be fairly certain that the likes of Chuck Berry would never become aware that their songs had been so drastically changed to suit a crusade that would quite possibly make them red in the face with anger.

The LP, Fetch the Rope, was well received in its targeted audience and added another string to Ian's bow. As expected The Klansmen were in great demand in the States, again the Klan requested Ian's services for a nation-wide tour. Although he hinted that this might be a possibility, privately he was reluctant to go on grounds of security. Ian genuinely felt that his life would be at risk on any Stateside visit. It was this fear that saw him refuse every opportunity to visit the north American continent.

Rock-o-rama demanded a constant flow of material and although this could be seen as a strain on Ian, he saw it as an opportunity to realise various aspirations. The next step was to release a solo album. With plenty of material available to him, he went to work on the No Turning Back LP. Thirteen tracks that resembled the bands' Hail the new dawn era, more than their later offerings. Ian had returned the hard edge that many staunch Skinheads had been crying out for. Happy with the carefully arranged compositions, Ian again ventured to Croydon. In the studio he was a man that just wanted to get down and do it, he couldn't be doing with all the fussing and endless time consumption that recording entails. As far as he was concerned he'd done his bit by writing the material, it was up to the studio to do the rest. In the hands of Scotty he could afford this outlook, in Croydon it was a different story. The studio was more used to recording radio jingles than it was rock bands. Situated at the end of a street of terraced houses, the owner hadn't attained the relevant planning permission for the studio and so had to be careful not to upset the neighbours. Because of this, all drumming sessions were conducted with a kit comprising of the usual drums minus the bass drum. In its place an electronic drum pad was set up. The affect of this was a distinctive clicking sound, where a heavy bass sound should have been. The engineers did their best to deliver the goods, but they were engineers and not producers. Some songs sounded better than others but many had a demo feel to them.

Inclued on No Turning Back are cover versions of Elvis Presley's 'In the Ghetto', The

Who's 'Behind Blue Eyes' and AC-DC's 'It's a hard Road', all given the Stuart treatment. His original compositions directed their venom at anything and everything left-wing.

*This time it's just a scuffle, well what can I say,*
*Put it all behind me for another day,*
*It's a daily battle, fight until the end,*
*Someday they'll realise I'm not gonna bend,*

*All out attack, Yeah, the courage we won't lack,*
*No Turning back, No turning back,*

*Heat is coming at us, we stand up strong,*
*Every other white man is trying to kill our song,*
*We won't fold before them, for there's no turning back,*
*Cowards will not beat us, the courage we won't lack,*

Whatever the outcome, their was only one road for Ian. The music had become his life, there really was no turning back. Being the lynch pin of the scene had its responsibilities

and, although he had no challengers for his position at the top, it meant that the pressure was his alone to deal with.

The only income he had came from record and T-shirt sales, but it was enough to keep him going. Not interested in material goods, it bothered him little that he was living in a tiny bedsit. Even when the ceiling started leaking and the only thing for tea was a large packet of cheese and onion crisps he never let it affect him.

A typical day for Ian Stuart was to rise at eight o'clock, collect the newspapers from the newsagents and flick through them over breakfast at his local cafe. At about eleven o'clock

he'd write a few letters, go over new songs on his acoustic guitar and the break for his daily intake of Soap operas. His favourite Soaps were Neighbours and Emmerdale farm of which he rarely missed. Mid-afternoon would see him visit his post office box in Holborn where he'd collect his mail and adjourn to a nearby cafe. Supporters wrote from all over the world, including Russia, Columbia, Brazil and Japan. New bands would send demo's and photo's in the hope of a mention in the next edition of Blood and Honour magazine. Ian received approximately twenty letters a day. After reading his mail, processing merchandise orders and banking the cheques, Ian would often relay his new material to close comrades via his acoustic guitar. Every other week day was spent in training, lifting weights and running. After being attacked while out running Ian resorted to running up and down the five flights of stairs in the bedsit. God only knows what his neighbours thought on opening their room doors to see the bulky Skinhead charging up and down the rickety wooden stairs. Most evenings were spent with visitors, listening to records. Ian had a vast collection of records, and although his guests were hoping to listen to the music of the RAC bands, Ian preferred rock music and would more likely have the latest Motorhead, Cult and Rolling Stones releases on the recoird player. When it came to alcohol Ian was only ever interested in Lager, and even then he would bemoan that it didn't taste like his beloved cups of tea. His evening meal was, more often than not, pie and chips.

# Chapter Nineteen
# Out in the cold

The upsurge of interest in RAC over the past couple of years had seen a growth in record sales and Rock-o-rama were keen to cash in. At this point quality really gave way for quantity. Almost anyone with enough strings on his guitar to make a sound was being offered a deal. Bands were sprouting up all over the place but most didn't make it past their first year.

In this climate Ian was being encouraged to produce at an enormous rate. The German label wanted Solo, Klansmen, and Skrewdriver LP's. Anything that bore the name Ian Stuart was hot commercial property in terms of the Skinhead boom. Rock-o-rama boss, Herbert Egoldt, had given Ian carte blanche to do as he wished. There was talk of a 'White blues' recording, and the possibility of Ian recording an album full of songs from various RAC bands, a sort of 'RAC greatest hits'. Ian was keen on almost all the ideas, especially the RAC compilation. Although he was master of Blood and Honour, in private he never had a lot of time for the music of his counterparts, with exception of the top groups. Ocean of Warriors by Brutal Attack and For You by Public Enemy were tracks that would have featured on the compilation, had the project ever got off the ground.

Priority would of course have to be given to Skrewdriver, and so Ian was back in Croydon laying down tracks for the new Warlord LP. Influenced by the choral effects on the latest Manowar offerings, Ian plumped for heavy backing vocals and so enlisted the help of various RAC front men. The effect worked well but again the studio let the show down. After the precision and quality of the previous three Skrewdriver LP's, there was much to live up to and Croydon just didn't seem to have it.

Warlord featured the usual subjects, the reds, the SS and white warriors of the past. Added to this was a couple of cover versions, Lynyrd Skynyrd's 'Simple Man' and AC DC's 'Back in Black', the former was the most successful of the two and became very popular in RAC circles. The LP closed on a stirring track about death, Ian's death and a future without him. Almost as if he could predict the future Ian had put into words his instructions to his disciples. Musically 'Suddenly' was the best track on the album and this added to its profound lyrics which are nothing short of a self-penned epitaph.

*We live in changing times,*
*Where certain thoughts are now a crime*
*Power flows through an evil pen,*
*And freedom's light is glowing dim*

*One day if suddenly I'm forced to take my leave*
*Will you still carry on with the things that we believe?*
*One day if suddenly they take my life away*
*Will you still be fighting to win a bright new day?*

*The people stood against us,*
*They seem to be above the law*
*With the power to listen in to private moments in our lives,*
*And the power to come kick down your door*

The Warlord LP was quickly followed up by, Ian's second solo effort, Slay the Beast. Again the last track on the album, Wall of Tears, was the best. All in all, the album fell short of a lot of Ian's achievements to date and his fans expectations. Quantity was again getting the better of quality. Luckily for Ian, and more so for Rock-o-rama, Ian was streets ahead of almost all of the competition on the RAC scene, so the decline in standards had less affect than it possibly should have. More and more cover versions were appearing on Ian's albums, many of them second rate. Slay the Beast was no exception with the inclusion of Golden Earring's 'Radar love' and a rather tame cover of the Stones''Sympathy for the Devil'.

With Cutdown shutdown and the Anti-Fascists getting more and more prominence in the media, decisions had to be made. The scene had gone a bit flat and in London the bubble really did seem to have burst. Recordings were coming out of the woodwork, but while almost every major RAC band was puting together their latest musical offerings, the live scene was falling by the wayside.

After the fight at the Tunnel Club, Skrewdriver's guitarist Ross had to watch himself. The Casuals had been totally embarrassed by the situation but knew they would have to some extent swallow over this one. These ex-Skinheads had no respect for the modern day generation of Skins but would not cut ties with the RAC scene completely. Ross was a marked man. He would be safe at gigs because the Casuals would not want a repeat of the incident at Greenwich but outside of the RAC arena he was fair game. Ross had found a few openings in the music business through various contacts and decided to move on, becoming a roadie for major rock bands such as The Cult.

With Ross gone, Ian would have to reorganise the group. Merv also threw the towel in opting for settling down to family life with his new wife. The new openings were filled by Lionheart Bassist 'Smiley Jon'. Taking up where Ross left off was Midlands based 'Stigger', to whom Ian was introduced by his sister Diane.

After the success of the first Klansmen LP with the Rock-a-billy scene, it was decided that the follow-up should be recorded. Again Ian found himself heading for Croydon with a new band of musicians, including two from another major pschobilly band. Rebel with a Cause was more laid back than usual Stuart compositions. The content and cover featured a cross-over theme of Rock-a-billy, the Klan and Bikers.

The Ku Klux Klan was receiving a lot of news coverage due to its growth in Britain. Crosses were being lit on a weekly basis all around England and southern Scotland. A major Hollywood blockbuster was released and featured a white supremacist theme. The film attracted many critics for not going hard enough on the racists. Tom Berenger took the starring role as an ex-soldier who was sick of multi-racialism and the degeneration of the major US cities and was fighting back with terror tactics with the help of a highly sophisticated network of racists across America. Betrayed was an immediate favourite among the right wing fraternity in London. The film makers gave enough sympathy and credence to Berenger's part to make it rise above the usual Hollywood 'thick Nazi' and 'outwitted racist degenerate' stereotypes.

The story of Betrayed was loosely based on the life of Robert Mathews, a white supremacist who formed the US terror group 'The Order'. Responsible for the death of a Jewish radio chat show host and the robbery of at least five million pounds from Brinks security trucks, The Order rose to infamy in the early Eighties. The organisation went to ground when the FBI caught various ring leaders and after they had cornered Bob Mathews in a farmhouse that they bombed out, killing Mathews in the process.

Robert Mathews became the Robin Hood of the right wing. He was highly respected because he put his words into action, something no-one had dared to do since the days of George Lincoln Rockwell. Ian Stuart added to the Mathews mythology with a song included on the Rebel with a cause LP entitled Gone with the Breeze.

*You're gone with the breeze, just like the leaves on the trees*
*Gone are the times with your family*

*You left life behind, You knew that your death warrant's signed*
*But there was no way you would compromise, No compromise*

*You're gone with the breeze*
*But you'll always be there on our minds*
*You're gone with the breeze*
*Just a memory of those times*

*You stood against lies, but you would never hide*
*You stood face to face with the enemy*
*Against all the odds, danger's path you trod*
*You knew it could only end in tragedy*

*All end in devastation, for a man who loved his nation*
*Another warrior that they took away*
*In our hearts he did not die, Forever more his flags we'll fly*
*And one day the land will honour his memory, Robert Mathews*

With his guitarist based in the Midlands and his bassist further north, the need for Ian to remain in the capital became less. The left were trapping his every move in London and his experience with the Chelsea fans at Kings Cross station was prompting him to up his belongings and head north. Most of the gigs were being held up north and the east Midlands was a very fertile place for Nationalism.

While living at his central London dwellings, Ian had found pickets standing outside his local Cafe, found leftists with placards outside his bedsit door, been confronted with closed door treatment from pubs and shops alike, not because they didn't like him, but out of fear of all he brought with him and reprisals from his enemies.

When some BNP supporters were embroiled in a bit of fisty cuffs with a mob of left-wingers the police pounced. On their release from the station they contacted Ian to say that the police had thought they were lefties and were asking them to identify Ian as one of the assailants. The police had allegedly told them they would do their best to rid London of this irritating racist.

To what extent this story was fiction or truth was not apparent, what was more important was that it was enough to push Ian over the edge. Many Nationalists who had endured spells at her Majesty's pleasure gave the impression that it was no problem. Ian detested his time in jail and was prepared to go to great lengths to avoid it. The BNP supporters story had certainly put the wind up him. "It got to the point where Commies were following me around every pub, they had demonstrations outside my house every three to four weeks. I wasn't bothered about the Commies, it was when the police tried to stitch me up. There's not a great deal you can do." Ian packed up his belongings and took the road up north.

Arriving in Ilkeston he stayed with the family of a Skinhead by the name of Cat. Ian and Cat then moved into a house in Copmanay. Ian knew the area from gigs he'd played in Ilkeston and the surrounding area, but what really struck him was how friendly everyone was. Of course there were a few star-struck Skins here and there, but for the most part everyone was genuinely welcoming.

Cat was well known in the area and had been a Skinhead for the best part of his life, the two hit it off well and eventually became as close as brothers.

The east Midlands would now become the focal point of Ian's struggles. No longer interested in the hassle and hounding of London life, almost all UK gigs would now be based in Nottinghamshire, Derbyshire or Staffordshire, with occasional jaunt to Newcastle. Ian became more relaxed about life although the band did suffer from the infrequent practices, but the increase in gigs gave them just enough sharpness to push on.

Gordon Jackson was a big fish in these parts. Ian had been introduced to him at earlier gigs and thought he was alright. A burley ex-grave digger, Gordy, as he was known, had taken up a position as bouncer, a position that served him well in his drive to recruit new members for the British Movement.

Often sceptical about Gordy, the BM kept him at a distance but allowed him to control the Nottingham division of their small grouping due to some success and the flood of recruits he had amassed. Ian had known some figures in the London BM and had previously appeared as a guest speaker at one of their meetings. Soon Gordy had persuaded Ian that he should work with the BM and allow them to organise his concerts, freeing up his time to concentrate on writing and recording new material. Ian was happy to go with the flow. He had no reason to mistrust Gordy but had not learned much from his previous experiences with the different factions of the NF. They always lasted a short while before doing a runner with the money. Ian was very trusting and perhaps more than a little naive at times.

The scene was flourishing in the Midlands and Ian rarely ventured out of the area. The exception was for European gigs. In the past Ian had made them few and far between, he hated travelling, but with a new feeling of security at his new base, he felt ready to take on the world. Germany became a familiar haunt, they worshipped him there and would queue around the block just to get his signature in the inside of their Flight jackets. Italy was the same, it was more than just fan meets Pop star scenario. To many of them Ian was a God.

Foreign gigs never went off without their own hassles though, and in Italy the venues were switched at the last minute, Police raided homes and the media went into Witch hunt mode. But still the organisers managed to pull it off with some success. Retorno Camelot proclaimed the heading of the flyer advertising Skrewdriver and host of Italian Fascist Skinhead groups. Italy had always been overshadowed by the success and power in Germany, but now as a scene it was really coming into its own.

Back in England, the control that Gordy had attained started to go to his head. Becoming like someone from a second rate Gestapo movie, he surrounded himself with a group of

Skinhead mobsters and in the name of the BM he would determine punishment beatings. On one occasion he went too far and a lad of twenty was bashed up for no real reason. Everyone was disgusted. The BM dis-owned him and Ian cut all ties.

Many Notts Skins found they were no longer welcome at Skrewdriver gigs. Tarnished with the brush of Gordy, they remained in no man's land for some time. For many it was a bitter pill to swallow.

Again Ian felt that he had been dumped on by a political party. The British Movement were no longer flavour of the month and he was soon swearing an allegiance to the British chapter of the Ku Klux Klan. As with his stints with the NF, BM etc. many Skinheads jumped on the bandwagon. Some were questioning the validity of it all. The Klan was steeped in American history and its relevance to the British people was relatively non-existent. To most Skinheads that didn't matter, they were anti-black and that was good enough for them.

Blood and Honour was now in the hands of a Skinhead by the name of Neil Parrish. Short and tubby, Parrish was immediately recognisable by the tear drop tattoos below his eyes. Ian didn't want the hassle so he handed him control of the magazine and his merchandise outlet Skrewdriver Services, in return for a monthly pay check.

Parrish had organised a few gigs in the Milton Keynes area and also some regular spots in Northampton. Parrish was keen to encourage some of the upcoming newcomers which included such bands as Battlezone, English Rose and even Celtic Dawn from Ireland.

The Black Lion pub in Northampton had welcomed its new trade. The pub had gone from being one of the quietest to the most profitable in the area. It wasn't long before trouble flared with a multi-racial group that frequented a nearby pub. A mob had surrounded a young Skinhead and his girlfriend and pulled knives on them. They managed to get away with a few cuts and bruises. On return to the Black Lion the news spread, exaggerated ten fold by the time one of the Milton Keynes Skinheads jumped on a table and theatrically declared the beginning of a race war. About twenty Skinheads rushed to the pub and within seconds the windows were put through, chairs were being thrown and everyone dispersed after the premises was sprayed with CS gas. The Skinheads returned victorious to the Black Lion and without much ado the gig began.

For weeks afterwards the Skinheads became focal point of much newspaper hysteria. One paper had the heading 'Town heading for riot'. Justin Saint, the owner of the Black lion knew that the Skinheads' number was up. He would have to say goodbye to his latest clientele and the massive profits they brought with them. "Skrewdriver are a racist band and we wouldn't entertain them here. We have had bands here, but it's just dancing and drinking." Mr Saint refused to admit to harbouring racists and said that the reason he'd stopped the shows was due to numbers. "A month ago we had four-to-five hundred Skinheads here and there was no trouble. The police said enough was enough, so we had to let it fall off."

If there was no trouble at Northampton, that certainly couldn't be said about a Skrewdriver concert in Birmingham. Tensions were high between a group of local Skinheads who followed local Oi band Close Shave and Skrewdriver Security. Bouncers at Skrewdriver gigs were made up of the hardest element of the bands following and had made a name for themselves way back in Nineteen eighty-two during the fight with Infa-riot. The tradition had been proudly carried on. On this night in Birmingham those present would witness Skrewdriver Security at their most violent. Predominantly from Ian's new home town and led by Cat, they were all approximately six foot tall and spent most of their spare time lifting weights.

Not long after Skrewdriver had come off stage there was a flash point and Security went into action. The bar staff immediately called for the police and on their approach they could see about thirty Skinheads going for it toe to toe. The local Skinhead crew were getting wiped out and the police had second thoughts about moving in, choosing to wait until things had died down before emptying the hall.

Skinheads had always protested that there was never trouble at gigs and for the best part this was true. Their reputation had got them thrown out of pubs and banned from hiring halls. But if violence wasn't a regular occurrence at gigs, Security had just proved that if anyone wanted it they were quite prepared to dole it out.

# Chapter Twenty
# Free my Band

Although there had been a glut of record releases, Nineteen ninety had been fairly quiet on the Blood and Honour scene in Britain. Brutal Attack had called it day after their guitarist Martin Cross was sent to prison after hitting his neighbour with an axe. No Remorse were off around the world playing gigs in America and Canada. Skullhead and Squadron were making a name for themselves on the continent. The main Nationalist parties had lost some of their prominence. Skrewdriver had recorded one of their weakest LP's in The Strong Survive. The move from Croydon to Nottingham recording facilities had done nothing to improve the sound. In the new LP they had attempted to add a dimension of Heavy Metal and it hadn't worked out. The guitar was thin and many of the songs wouldn't have made it out of the Stuart song book a few years back. To top it all, it came in a cheap looking, badly drawn black and white cover. If White Rider had been an album to remember then Strong Survive was surely one to forget.

Nineteen ninety-one started in much the same vein. There were the rucks at Birmingham and Northampton, but apart from that the RAC scene was invisible to the public eye.

Ian was putting himself before the band for the first time in a long while and he was enjoying it. Nightlife was good, a lot of the local pubs knew and welcomed him by name, he would often frequent Nottingham's Heavy metal Night club Rock City. Learning to drive had proved easier than he'd thought and Ian was soon a proud owner of a Volkswagen Golf, chosen probably because of Volkswagen's links to the Third Reich. The leader of Blood and Honour couldn't afford to be seen driving anything other than a European car. Ian had also found himself a steady girlfriend in Diane Calladine, the sister of his guitarist Stigger.

Diane was one of maybe three or four girlfriends that he had taken seriously in his life, so much so that later in the year he announced his engagement to her. They visited his family home in Blackpool where the news was greeted with some relief that perhaps he wouldn't walk so close to the edge. The two went off to Yugoslavia on a package holiday, probably the first holiday of Ian's adult life. Ian hated the experience and came back with tales of rats running around the hotel. And the sound of gunfire in the distance.

Not everyone was happy about the union. Many locals thought that she was just using him for the gifts he showered her with, and that she was distracting him from his mission in life. The relationship was not always smiles and roses and was often as much off as it was on. Underneath there must have been something between them because he was never short of admirers but he always yearned for Diane.

With the boom in Europe Skrewdriver were still very much a marketable commodity and the pressure remained to satisfy the demands of Rock-o-rama. A live LP was planned and took place in Burton on Trent and, although it was miles better than the bootleg 'We've got the power' produced in Nineteen eighty-eight, it didn't capture the atmosphere that helped the band remain the number one racist band in the world. Recorded on a Saturday lunchtime, the audience were too sober to get into it, and so as not to waste the opportunity, the sound effect of a clapping audience was added to the live soundtrack. Live and Kicking the title, the double LP came with a gate sleeve featuring pictures of various members of Skrewdriver and their crew.

High on the success of the previous years concert, the Italian Skins were again planning a concert, and so in August Skrewdriver were back on stage at the Retorno Camelot. Again police action had failed to stop the event, but the aftermath was hard to take for many of the assembled fascists. For weeks after the concert police arrested dozens of leading figures on the Italian RAC scene. With many on the authorities curfew, the movement was immediately de-railed.

Keen to expand on the success of the Klansmen Ian again ventured into the studio to record a Rock LP under the name of White Diamond. The attempt was to draw on the Biker audience that had shown some interest in Skrewdriver. A local drummer and a bassist were recruited to join Ian and Stigger. The Reaper, as the album was called, was a dismal effort. There was a lack of conviction in the voice of Ian as he mulled over the non-committal lyrics to the backing of fairly tame rock guitar.

"The Klansmen brought a lot of Rock-a-billies into the Blood and Honour Movement, which is a good thing." Ian told Blood and Honour magazine. "Hopefully the White Diamond will do the same thing for Bikers. Basically we are spreading our wings and trying to appeal to everybody - not just Skinheads."

Any negative come back Ian received for White Diamond didn't falter his appetite to try new things and again Ian returned to the same Meadow farm Studios to record an album of acoustic songs entitled Patriotic Ballads.

Those who were unhappy with his previous efforts would find relief in the Ballads LP. With no need for technical wizardry the striking vocals could rest easy on the backing acoustic guitar. The LP took no longer than two days to record, almost Johnny Cash style. One man and his guitar. The album featured versions of the popular gig stomp Tomorrow Belongs to me, as well as the ballad Suddenly and The Snow fell along with some new compositions Who cares? and White blues.

As the scene grew more and more stale in England, Europe became the new focal point of activities. Germany was going through a resurgence both politically and on the Skinhead

# ROCK BAND HELD IN NAZI RIOT SWOOP

FIVE British skinheads arrested in Germany following the stabbing of a youth in a riot are members of fanatical neo-Nazi rock band Skrewdriver.

## Brit group seized as armed mob go on rampage

## BRIT SKINHEADS HELD IN NAZI BATTLE

### Germans try to extradite skinheads from Britain

### gang join Germans

### Race hate attacks on hostel

### Extradition of Britons sought

### Brit skins held over Nazi battle

front. Unification in Nineteen eighty-nine had brought an influx of immigrants in on top of

the burden of rebuilding the East. The German people were not happy. It was a very fertile ground for the right wing. Political groups popped up everywhere and the difference was that they were prepared to work with one another. Together they realised they were a real force to be reckoned with. Immigrant hostels became targets as German youths vented their anger, often encouraged by their elders. The country was in a very volatile state.

Skrewdriver received an invitation to play at an anniversary concert for the unification of Germany. The concert would be staged at Werben on the third of October. Werben is near Cottbus, inside what was previously East Germany close by to the border with Poland. Ian agreed and the Deutsche Alternative group set about organising the event.

Ian had been well aware of the situation in Germany, this was also reflected in his latest recordings. Tracks that would feature on the next Skrewdriver album Freedom, What Freedom? included One Land about the re-unification and Stolz, a song sung in German about German pride. The album was a distinct improvement on Strong Survive which had been heralded in some quarters as the beginning of the end for the band.

On arriving in Germany the band were given a warm welcome and, with a few days to go before the concert, there was plenty of time for drinking and partying. With members of the most famous White Power band present, some locals, fired up on beer, thought they'd prove their dedication. What started off as high spirits soon turned ugly when Skinheads attacked a youth club. The club was often used as a meeting place for socialist groups. All of a sudden the air was thick with violence, baseball bats were being wielded and a long-haired, twenty year-old man was stabbed.

When the police arrived on the scene they immediately picked up who they could and arrested them. For the locals it was a regular occurrence, for the Brits it was a bad situation, not knowing the streets. Among the six arrested five were British, four of them from the band.

At the time of the incident Ian was asleep with his girlfriend in an apartment, totally oblivious to what had gone on. He and Diane had plumped for an early night and so went off leaving the others to a night of drinking.

In the middle of the night Ian was woken by the sound of hammering on the front door. Before he had time to get up and enquire who it was, the police had burst into his room and were pointing guns at his head.

Unlike western Germany, in the eastern parts virtually no-one spoke English and so it wasn't until he was taken to the police station did he find out what was going on. After about six hours both Ian and Diane were released. The remaining members of his band were not so fortunate.

What started off as a small incident had turned into a serious cause for alarm. About three hundred Skinheads had gathered, tooled-up with knives, bats and pistols and were intent on freeing the captives. For a while the police station was under seige with the police barricaded inside. Eventually, after fifty arrests, order was restored.

Wilfried Robineck, the local prosecutor was moving fast to make arrangements to move the six to the high security Moabit Jail in Berlin. "As long as they are in Cottbus there will be trouble. We expect our Skinheads to start fighting in protest over their arrests." The papers were full of it.

The incident couldn't have come at a worse time for the six. A Ghanian had been burned to death in a racist attack the previous week. Police were on red alert over the past month as incidents of racist outbursts were growing at an alarming rate. The world's media was homing in and the Government were under heavy pressure to come up with answers.

The British tabloid press were quick to pick up on the situation. Reports were claiming links had been set up for British Nazis to join up with their counterparts in Germany to start a race war. Although it was true to say that Skrewdriver were there to bolster the racist cause, the organisation that the press were reporting on was far too complex and far fetched.

Garry Bushell was quick to put the boot in. "Swastika junkies like Skrewdriver disgrace our flag and our country, they even manage to disgrace Skinheads." In his column in The Daily Star he ranted "If they love the Krauts so much why don't they move there for good?"

The prisoners were certainly in the wrong place at the wrong time. But the press would hear none of Ian's "Scapegoats" theory. They had their prey and were determined to go in for the kill.

In Berlin, the six would see the harsh reality of German Prison life. The jail was full of Turkish criminals and no-one spoke English. They were split up and the one visit they were allowed, had to be monitored with the visitors asked to speak slowly so that the German prison officer could decipher what was being said.

Back in Cottbus the police were expecting trouble. The concert went ahead with four hundred police drafted in to control the two thousand Skins that had travelled from all over Germany. Ian was backed up by Stuerkraft, a top selling Skinhead band of their time. Ian was given a rapturous applause when he took the stage and blasted his way through the Skrewdriver set changing the words of 'Voice of Britain' to 'Voice of Deutschland' and 'Free my land' to 'Free my band'.

As the plane touched down on home soil Ian was pleased to be back in Britain, but the ordeal hadn't dampened any thoughts of going back. Angry with what he saw as unjust treatment he told Skinhead fanzine Last Chance "I don't know about the rest of the band, but me personally, It's made me want to go out there and cause a lot more trouble. The way I see it is that Skrewdriver are being made scapegoats for the fact that the German Government have brought in too many immigrants into the country."

Ian set to work on a protest recording and gathered some local musicians who promptly recorded a six track mini-LP titled Ian Stuart and Rough Justice - Justice for the Cottbus six. The tracks were non-political bar the title track.

*And the people call for justice, "Justice"*
*And none of your dirty little tricks*
*Yeah, the people call for justice, "Justice"*
*And that means freedom for the Cottbus six*

*Within four evil walls, accused of a crime*
*And all they'd done is be in the wrong place at the wrong time*
*Doing all that we can to free innocents*
*But our hands are tied by the lying press and corrupt governments*

With no evidence to go on, the five Britons were finally released before Christmas, and prior to the release of the Cottbus mini-LP. All five were Banned from Germany. Ian managed to persuade Smiley and Stigger to remain in the group, but for Drummer Jon it was too much and he quit. He had been with the band over four years and decided enough was enough. Ian would have to find someone else to back him on his trips to 'the Fatherland'. For the short term Stoerkraft and Noie Werte were happy to help out.

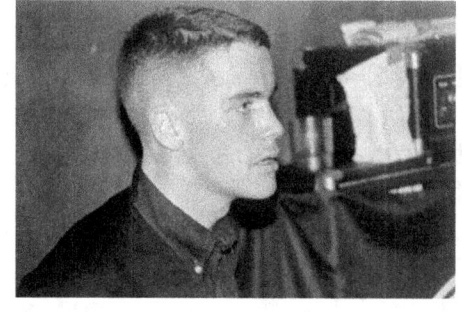

Again the media were interested in Blood and Honour and Skrewdriver in particular. TV programmes were begging to get into gigs but it was the same old story when they did. On interviewing the Skrewdriver security boss, Cat was asked if he wanted another drink every five minutes, and although he wasn't aversed to an evening of free beer, he was very aware of the plan. He called their bluff much to their embarrassment.

# Chapter Twenty-One
# Betrayed

Nicky Crane, once the mere mention of his name would bring fear rushing to the heart of his enemies and pride to his supporters. A Skinhead muscle man with a reputation for violence.

A leading light in the right-wing, some time before Skrewdriver's reformation in the early eighties, Crane was Based in South East London where he ran the Crayford branch of the British Movement. Craney, as he was known to his mates, was singing in the semi-fascist band the Afflicted who performed such compositions as White boy and I'm afflicted to a regular Skinhead crowd in New Cross.

In Nineteen eighty-one he received a four year prison sentence for his part in a race riot in Woolwich in which a Black gang was ambushed getting off a train and running battles ensued.

It was while in jail that Crane received his recognition. When a concert by the Four-Skins erupted in a riot involving Southall's large Asian community, Skinhead concert goers and Police, the media went crazy looking for someone to hang.

Accompanying the pictures of burnt out cars and Police vans outside the charred remains of the Hanborough Tavern was a story of how the right-wing had set Oi up as a trojan horse. Devised to recruit for the very kind of race riots that had been experienced on the streets of West London.

Oi had been adopted and promoted by Garry Bushell who had compiled, on behalf of Sounds magazine, an EMI compilation LP featuring some Punk and Skinhead bands along with Cockney poets and Football terrace chants. On the follow up to the highly successful Oi the album, he was again involved in compiling the tracks, and while their wasn't a trace of racism to be found within the music, the choice of cover model was enough to feed the Witch hunt.

The 'Strength thru Oi' LP cover featured a picture of Nicky Crane - Boots, braces and

British Movement tattoos. The press were quick to expose the 'Thug on the cover'. For Crane the exposure was something he was not at all bothered about. It was just another cutting to add to the scrapbook that he kept. For outsiders it was just another notch on his reputation, he was certainly not someone to mess about with.

An obvious recruit for Skrewdriver security he joined up on his release and immediately took control. Not only had he terrorised the streets of south east London but his reputation earned him the respect of east London Skinheads whom he rallied for a battle at Jubilee gardens in the June of Nineteen eighty-four. The British Movement had gone before him and attacked the stage holding Skrewdriver rivals the Redskins, but Crane stole the headlines. Pictures of him and his crew flattening the stage where Hank Wangford were per-

forming appeared in the following days newspapers. Although Crane was easily identifiable, no action was taken against him.

In Nineteen eighty-six Crane received six months for a fight on a tube train. He had previously got out of another scrape when he turned up in court wearing a suit, bow tie and permed wig. Everyone was laughing. He looked like Kevin Keegan, but Crane insisted it was due to baldness. Even the judge laughed. He wasn't so lucky the second time around.

When Blood and Honour hit the headlines at the beginning of Nineteen eighty-eight Crane was back again in his familiar security role. It was about this time that rumours were circulating that Crane had been seen at Gay events and that he was a closet homosexual.

Ian was having none of it. He had been given no reason to believe the allegations. Crane had done a good job for the band, both as Chief of security and as cover artist for Hail the New Dawn and After the Fire. Working for protection agency, Gentle touch, Crane was able to shrug off any connection with the London Gay scene as 'just part of his security work'.

From Nineteen eighty-nine onwards Crane dropped out of sight. Security was safely in

Cat's hands and London was no longer the Skinhead hive of activity it once was. Many people put it down to the fact that Ian was no longer in the Capital.

The end of July Nineteen ninety-two would deliver an unwelcome surprise to Ian, Blood and Honour and the right wing movement as a whole. First in the Independent, under the heading 'Reformed fascist ready to admit homosexuality' Crane confessed. "They are in for a hell of a shock. I always wanted to come out, it was a difficult decision, I was so well known." It was reported that Crane was now a big figure in the flourishing Gay Skinhead fashion scene. "A lot of

Skinheads will feel betrayed by me and I will be a target for physical attacks but my stand may help others."

He was not wrong about the physical threat. That weekend members of the British Movement Leader Guard, to which Crane once belonged, were scouring the streets of central London looking for him. If they'd have found him it's probable that the results would have been fatal. They issued a statement among their small production of newsletters that Crane had disgusted them and 'brought the name of British Movement into disrepute'.

The Sun latched on to the story giving it a full page prominence. 'Nazi Nick is a PANZI' read the headline, accompanied by photo's of Crane as he was previously known in a White Power T-shirt and wielding an axe in a pose for magazine shoot from some years back. In the Sun he shed some light on his life of violence and hiding his big secret. "I knew I had homosexual feelings, but I used to stifle them. In the end I felt like a hypocrite carrying on in the right wing because the movement was so anti-gay, I was a fraud." Nicky Crane went on to say that Homosexual gangster Ronnie Kray was a great inspiration in tough times.

Ian was in Belgium at the time the story broke. Crane had used what contacts he had left to find out and call him there. He apologised to Ian and said that Searchlight had been on to him for information. He promised Ian that he'd not betray him or his racist beliefs, but although he never slammed the phone down on him, Ian just said "yeah, right" and that was it. The two would never talk again. "He left and that's the best thing he could do, but he should have left a lot earlier." Ian vented his anger to anyone who'd listen. "It just goes to show that Nationalism and Homosexuality don't go together. Homosexuality is a perversion."

A few days after Crane's revelations, Channel Four broadcast a programme titled Out - Fascist or Fetish, in which Crane and various other Homosexuals explained why they were drawn to the image of the Skinhead. Psychologists proclaimed that it was a form of defense, dressing up like their oppressor. Black Gays were worried about the trend, although Mr Crane told of how on one occasion a black man had followed him into the toilet to ask if he could lick Crane's boots. For your average Blood and Honour Skinheads this was too much to take. Many took to the streets and attacked Gay bars.

The next issue of Blood and Honour covered the story and Ian's White Whispers column was direct. 'Some of these creatures boasted of their first experiences with other men. It was enough to make you sick. Keep away from our movement for your own sake'. It had become quite chic in the Gay community to dress up in boots jeans and short hair. Just as in the eighties they had dressed as bikers, now they were dressing like Skinheads.

Underneath the anger, most of the Skinheads felt a deep sense of betrayal. No-one felt as betrayed as Ian who was very vocal on the subject. "I want nothing to do with him whatsoever, as far as I'm concerned he has dug his own grave." A lot of Skins had grown up with Strength thru Oi posters on their bedroom walls. Crane was an icon, and Skinheads didn't have many. He featured in Skins fanzine as 'Super Skin number one'. At one point he even had his own line of T-shirts which included such provocative designs as 'Strength thru Oi', 'Action man eighty' and 'Better dead than Red'. He seemed to be everything a Skinhead was supposed to be about, even his soft tone of voice hadn't bolstered any suspicions.

Eighteen months after the revelations, Crane was dead. He had contracted AIDS and slowly wasted away. The Skinhead fraternity met the news of his death with a great deal of silence. The scars were still there and the name Nicky Crane was erased from the hall of fame, in the vain hope of forgetting he ever existed.

It was quite possible that Crane was aware of his illness when he made the confessions, and perhaps it was his shame at living a lie that had made him determined not to die a martyr to a cause that would crucify his true self.

# Chapter Twenty-Two
# Waterloo Sunset

With the scene in Britain falling apart, London based organisers of Blood and Honour decided to put on a show that would eclipse all previous events. Concerts in Europe were far more successful than those held in England and many in the movement were growing tired of driving two hundred miles to see the same faces at the same small venues.

The twelfth of September was chosen as the date of the gig. Immediately efforts were made to advertise the concert on a scale not seen since the Main Event gig of three years previous. Posters, featuring a pair of doctor martin boots with the words 'Skrewdriver back in London' emblazoned across them, were put up all over the UK. Blood and Honour supporters pasted them up everywhere and local media in Newcastle, Bristol, Birmingham, Nottingham and even Glasgow were picking up on it.

The meeting point was Waterloo railway station in Central London. Within a matter of days of the news of the concert, all kinds of groups were calling for the event to be stopped. Everything was going to plan. Some people had reservations about the openness of the event, but they were persuaded that something had to be done to rejuvenate the fading scene. Anyone who was anyone in the RAC movement would know about it, and so there was no excuse for not showing. The news was spreading like wild fire across Europe. Although there were concerts being held more frequently and successfully on the continent, there was something about Britain that the Europeans all admired. Perhaps it was the fact that most of the major bands hailed from the UK. Perhaps the draw was the respect they all felt for the birth place of the Skinhead movement. What ever it was, there was a massive interest in the concert from overseas. The media were saying that it was a British show of force to the racists in Germany who had risen to such prominence over the last few years.

As expected the Anti-Fascists were planning a counter demonstration, and by chance they had the perfect opportunity to boost their ranks. Two weeks prior to the gig a big left-wing festival was taking place in East London. AFA took the opportunity to rally everyone there for the coming confrontation.

The concert organisers had concentrated on securing the hall and keeping security tight about the location of the venue, even Ian Stuart was prevented from knowing its whereabouts. The British Movement Leader Guard were drafted in to secure the venue. Their involvement was sure to put off some leading Combat 18 members who were finding it easy to operate among the Blood and Honour scene, but knew they couldn't take liberties at a BM policed event. Combat 18 had attempted to pull in people from the NF, BNP and KKK with some success, but when it came to the British Movement they found a closed door. Unlike some groups, the BM couldn't just be pushed aside.

Assemble:
Saturday 12th September 1992 at 4.30pm
Waterloo BR
(Bring a Travelcard)

A few days before the event the national press picked up on the story. 'Secret Nazi Pop show set to fan race hate' proclaimed the Daily Star. There was much confusion about the change of tactics, but everyone was forecasting trouble. Ian Stuart appeared on London LBC radio where he was interviewed by Richard Little-John. Ian played down the trouble aspect stating that he only wanted to play his music to his supporters and wished that he could be left alone to get on with it. Little-John responded by wishing him well.

Ian and the band met up with Blood and Honour organisers at a motorway service station. Before setting off to Eltham in south east London, news was coming through of trouble at Waterloo. Kirk Barker, Chief of Security, had been arrested on his arrival at Waterloo station, he held the key to security and it was unsure whether it was a mark of good police work or whether they just got lucky. Either way he was out of the picture, causing some confusion among the assembling Skinheads.

Before re-grouping the Skinheads had sustained two charges by a mob of Left-wing activists, bottles and bricks raining in from everywhere. Back on Waterloo bridge the Skinheads met up with some Casuals who were also heading for the concert. Surprising the demonstrators gathered in front of them, the racists charged and managed to regain some ground before the Police moved in to separate the factions. All trains to and from Waterloo were cancelled. Waterloo Bridge was brought to a stand still during the running

battles. One Policeman on the scene told the Press "It was like Custars last stand."

Two policemen were hospitalised, thirty three arrests were made, of which most were from the demonstrators, and two cars were badly damaged. The incident made the national news.

Back in Eltham arrangements were going ahead to start the concert. Search parties were sent out to find groups of stragglers who were touring the area trying to find the venue. It was estimated that there was about two thousand racists in London to see the concert. The biggest showing for an RAC event in Britain. Only a quarter of that made it to the venue. Those who did found Ian at his best. It may have been hard for him to get psyched up for a gig in Nottingham on a saturday afternoon, but he was ready to explode at this one. He blamed the police for going easy on the demonstrators.

The two other bands on the bill were No Remorse and Dirlewanger from Sweden, both bands had just returned from playing in California the previous day.

There was no way anyone was going to steal the show from Ian. He was fired-up and ready to go. It was a performance not seen in years. The police had asked that the bar be closed and at one point it was thought that the Police were going to raid the place. Outside they were lined-up in riot gear with CS Gas at the ready. Security boarded up the doors and after a dangerously tense few minutes the bar was re-opened taking the heat out of the situation.

On stage Ian let loose. Every song was preceded by a tirade against the Police, the demonstrators and the Left wingers who had physically attacked him in Nottingham the previous night. "Last night we were in a pub and a gang of niggers walked in. The first one glassed me and said 'Right the gig's off you Nazi bastard'. Is the gig off? - Is it Fuck!" Whipping the crowd into a frenzy, he continued. "Now we've got the police telling us it's off. Who's orders are those bastards taking? British and European people here to see a concert, down the road Public Enemy are saying kill Whitey - they're allowed to play. You've got the Pogues saying Up the IRA - they're allowed to play. So why are the pigs telling us we're not allowed to play. Fuck 'em - This one's called Tomorrow belongs to me." Again the music starts up, speakers booming out this Nazi anthem, being sung like it's the last thing the singer is ever going to do. Everyone present is taking note. The sheer intensity of Ian's verbal onslaughts are met with a response of Sieg Heil, arms raised in time to the beat of the drums.

If the organisers of the concert had planned to liven things up a bit then I'm sure they hadn't bargained on this. The event was featured on television and newspaper reports from Los Angeles to Greece and from Australia to Germany. The British press had a field day. 'Battle of Waterloo' was the title of almost every article.

Both sides claimed a victory and I suppose in the light of day the Left had made their presence felt at Waterloo, but Blood and Honour had successfully held the concert against massive odds. "This has got to stop before it gets out of hand." Said Mick Stone of Anti-Fascist Action in The Echo. "The fact that they have advertised the concert is a show of the Neo-Nazis increasing confidence." Jon Heddon, also of AFA told the same paper that "There was two hours of chaos. The Police presence was badly planned and there was a lot of confusion."

The event had thrown up the debate of how to contain the bootboys on the streets, but also the whole concept of racist music came into question. Tony Parsons, a long time

# BATTLE OF WATERLOO

## Hundreds clash on station's concourse

RUNNING battles between neo-Nazis and left-wing protesters brought chaos to south London streets at the weekend, as 200 police struggled to keep the two sides apart.

Tube and train services were disrupted at Water-

by MARK SYLVESTER

loo Station and the nearby South Bank complex became a battleground on Saturday afternoon when around 500 anti-fascists and 150 right-wingers clashed.

Turn to page 2

music critic, wrote "Oi as played by Skrewdriver and their kind is punk without the theatrical overtones, punk without O levels, punk that has never been to art school. This is the genuine voice of council estates. Real working class music. Unlike every musician since Elvis, Oi bands don't play with the mythology of danger. They were and are the real thing. It isn't pretty."

Ian and most RAC bands disliked the reference to Oi, as in their eyes they were Skinhead rock bands and Oi was too close to punk. Bands like Skrewdriver proved that there was some truth in their claims, but most RAC bands played Oi music and were closer to punk than rock.

33 charged after battle of Waterloo

Arm of the law: police lead away a demonstrator at Waterloo station where neo-Nazis clashed with anti-fascists and 44 people were arrested

Kirk Barker head of security received a three hundred pound fine but was remanded to face violent disorder charges relating to a Skinhead fight with Indians after a Buntingford gig the previous year.

The Guardian reported that another concert was being planned in Folkestone, Kent. This was a bit of a red herring. In reality none of the major bands had agreed to play and it really hadn't got passed the planning stages. The press lapped it up. There were futile demonstrations and the local press was full of fears that right-wing terrorists from the continent were going to be flooding the Sea Port town.

A spokesman for Blood and Honour was feeling hard done by but defiant about the future. "We will carry on regardless. The Communists organise concerts all the time. We organise a concert and the Jews, the Left-wing and government try to stop it - so much for democracy."

Ian Stuart told Last Chance fanzine "It was a shame that the Police acted so illegally again by shutting down the mainline train station and trying to stop people from getting to the concert. They should not have allowed the Left wing demonstration on the day because it was obvious they were only there to cause trouble".

For months after the event disputes were raging on the Blood and Honour scene about whether the concert should have been more low key. Many people asked why Combat 18 failed to show at Waterloo. Whatever the situation it certainly put Blood and Honour back on the map.

# Chapter Twenty-Three
# 1992 - The Year of Treachery

After Waterloo an entire debate was thrown up to discuss the legality of the RAC records and organisations such as Blood and Honour. MTV devoted a whole weekend to the subject. An open forum was set up comprising of musicians and political activists. Appearing on the show was Angelic Upstarts singer Mensi.

Mensi had penned one of the most patriotic Skinhead anthems of the late seventies. Ian Stuart had even been quoted as saying he wished he'd written 'England'. That was where the praise stopped. Ian hated Mensi with a vengeance, he was often attacked in the pages of Blood and Honour for his association with Anti-Fascist action. The two would use their concerts as a platform to slander one another.

Mensi was joined on the MTV show by the front man of another Anti-Nazi band, The Blaggers. One of the conditions of the two appearing on MTV was that the show would not allow a platform for the views of racists. For this reason the show was pathetically unbalanced. Left-wingers shouted down anyone even slightly questioning their stand, and at one point it veered from the subject of racism to some of the guests views about the IRA.

Around the same time AFA had been given a free hand to produce their own TV programme on BBC2. The show provoked a lot of controversy for its pro-violence stance. The group had not held anything back and were filmed, with faces covered, talking about violence being the only real method of flushing out the fascists. Ex-Boxer Terry Marsh was also featured on the programme and gave his backing to the group, who were also filmed attacking a small group of National Front supporters selling papers in Bermondsey. Marsh went on to become a Liberal election candidate after being dropped by the Labour party, but his appearance added some credibility to the anti-racists.

As far as Blood and Honour were concerned their enemies were having it all their own way. Without the opportunity to answer back they felt that their right to free speech had been denied them. As with other examples of this, they used it as propaganda to re-enforce, in their view, the conspiracy against them.

During the MTV weekend, the music channel reported from, among other places, Canada. The White Power Skins of Canada were becoming a big force. Bands such as The Cross and Rahowa had made a great deal of ground over the last few years. Rahowa was led by Church of the Creator minister George Hawthorne. The difference between Rahowa and their contemporaries was they could really play and had a fair deal of imagination when composing their songs. Not only was Hawthorne deeply involved in the political world of the North American right-wing, he was also instrumental in the formation of

Resistance records.

Based in Detroit, Resistance outshone Rock-o-rama by the quality of their products. Gone were the cheap black and white, one sided CD covers, replaced by carefully arranged artwork from top of the range designer Apple computers. The organisation also produced a full colour magazine to rival anything appearing on the shelves of WH Smith. The only label anywhere near them was Nordland in Sweden who also produced a similar magazine, written entirely in Swedish.

Blood and Honour magazine had picked up on the MTV debate and spared four pages to cover the subject. In Germany, a Skinhead band by the name of Radikhal were fined ten thousand pounds for producing records promoting National Socialism. It is illegal in Germany to promote any Nazi ideas and Radikhal's song, Hakenkreuz, (Swastika in English) called for the nobel peace prize to be awarded to Adolf Hitler. None of the British bands were affected by the clampdown and Ian Stuart went to great lengths to proclaim the legality of his records. "We are not actually banned over here. The newspapers say that we are so that the record shops won't stock them." Ian Stuart was angry about what he saw as music industry hypocrisy concerning Axl Rose from mega-rich rock group Guns and Roses. G'N'R produced an album that included the song 'One in a million' in which Axl slags off black hustlers and immigrants. "He can get away with saying the naughty N word (Nigger), because he's a druggie with a black in his band. I can't say the N word, unless of course, I smoke a joint and get a Rastafarian bass player. That's how fucked up and hypocritical everything is".

*Police and Niggers get out of my way*
*I don't need to buy none of your gold chains today*
*Don't need no bracelets slapped around my back*
*Just need some time now, won't you cut me some slack*
*Immigrants and Faggots, don't make no sense to me*
*They come to our country and think they'll do as they please.*

The music media had picked up on One in a million, and Geffen, Guns'n'roses record company, were panicking about lost millions if it all went wrong. Axl made a statement apologising for the offending lyrics, stressing that they were not about all blacks just the hustlers. The fuss soon died down and the album is still on sale today in all major record shops.

Blood and Honour also picked up on the Rap industry. Some black music had gone much further that the racists in calling for the killing of the police and attacking white people. Rap's anti-police, Anti-Gay and often anti-white message had not gone un-noticed. The music press handled the situation with kid gloves, afraid to offend the black community, it was a fear they loathed. The major record labels followed suit and Time Warner issued a statement. 'We have an obligation to ensure the voices of the powerless, the disenfranchised and those at the margins are heard'. Of course theirs was a decision made out of finance and not compassion. The black Rap market in the US was enormous and too lucrative for big business to pass up on.

Chief Blood and Honour organiser, Neil Parrish, awoke on the fifteenth of October to find that a picture of his house had been published and was listed as the headquarters of a terrorist organisation in the London Standard. His full address appeared forcing him to move his family out fearing attacks from the left. He was puzzled as to how the newspaper had got his address. Thinking that it could have possibly come from Keith Thompson, who had a reputation for talking to the press, he contacted him. Thompson, leader of the self styled League of St. George, was unmoved by the news. "Don't worry about it" he said. "They put me in there all the time. It's a sign to other nationalists that you are actually doing something." Not the slightest bit of sympathy for his wife and two small children was shown. After attaining some legal advice, Parrish decided that it would be too costly to make an action against the newspaper, although according to legal advisers he could have done well out of it.

In the wake of his newspaper appearance Parrish was expected to step up security, in reality he did quite the opposite. When Photojournalist Leo Regan was scouting the Skinhead scene for a lead in a publishing project Parrish agreed to a starring role and featured heavily in pictures and quotes in the resulting 'Public Enemies' book.

The spotlight of media attention was shining down from many quarters. TV Production companies were writing in, requesting permission to film concerts or interview some of the leading figures in Blood and Honour. Area five productions contacted Parrish to request a representative of B&H joined them on 'Project Journey'. The programme makers wanted to film a British racist taking a journey from London to France, to meet up with a French fascist, and then on to Germany, where they'd join Dutch and Germany nazi's, to discuss their beliefs. The venue for the filmed discussion was Auschwitz concentration camp. Since the latest TV programmes on the Right had treated its subject with such contempt, B&H bosses viewed Television enquiries with a sense of mistrust and tended to recline these offers. Project Journey found someone in the Scottish BNP to agree to comply, and so the show went on, but as a concept, it was something of a flop.

Back in Nottingham relations between Ian and some BM Skinheads in the area had began to improve. In the initial split after the ructions with Gordy, some of the Skins had received death threats from the Klan, but these were pretty poor efforts and the recipients would often laugh at the bad spelling. At the Waterloo concert a biker friend pulled Ian to one side and told him that things should be sorted out, a long time had passed and the lads no longer held any loyalty for Gordy, who was rumoured to be drug dealing in the Midlands. Ian agreed and used the White Christmas gig in Mansfield as the perfect opportunity to iron out past differences. Ian had long since drifted from the Klan and welcomed the move.

The Mansfield concert was a great success for Blood and Honour and when Skinheads took a slating in the local press, the organisation responded by accusing the local MP, Alan Meale, of double standards. A Rave concert had ended abruptly when a youth was rushed to hospital due to drugs mis-use, Windows were smashed and the police had a battle to retain order. At the White Christmas gig there was no trouble at all. The newspaper gave a great deal of space to the issue, asking 'Should we worry about the rise of nationalism in Mansfield?', quoting large chunks from the Blood and Honour magazine. Mr Meale said "If they want a white Christmas then I suggest they go to the north pole where they can taint as few people as possible with their evil views." Local press were usually more generous with the space they gave to stories concerning the far right. Racists tended to get more of the free speech they so desperately yearned for from the local rags. Local journalists tended to stick to the principles that their interviewees would hang themselves with their own words. They were often right. Ian was pleased with the outcome, the coverage had drawn Blood and Honour to the attention of more people and boosted the recruitment drive in the area.

While on a trip to Blackpool with Diane, Ian became embroiled in a dispute with a man at a night club. Diane was complaining that the man was getting a little over friendly with his her and when he turned up again at a chip shop Ian let him have it. It was not a serious fight, certainly not by Ian's standards, but the police arrested them all the same. On being released Ian was surprised to hear that he would have to return to face charges. Again Ian put this down to a conspiracy to silence him. Ian was well known in Blackpool and the local paper often gave him a few inches of newsprint every time he was in the area. Writing for the Gazette since Skrewdriver's early days, Mark Benattar was a journalist who had attempted to keep tabs on Blackpool's very own musical Hitler.

More bad news for Ian was on the horizon. The monthly cheque from Skrewdriver services seemed to be getting smaller and smaller, at a time when business was good, mainly due to the publicity of Waterloo. Then suddenly Neil Parrish disappeared. His phone was out, there was no sign of him in Milton Keynes and un-surprisingly the money was gone too. Ian was furious. His monthly bundle amounted to at least four hundred pounds of tax free cash, but more importantly Parrish had left orders amounting to six thousand pounds worth of goods that had not been honoured. Charlie Seargent of Combat 18 stepped in and said he'd help. Somehow he managed to collect left over stock from Parrish's house and promised he'd forward the money once he'd sold them through his fanzine The Order. It is very doubtful whether the orders were ever honoured, but Ian did send out letters warning people of Parrish's actions. C18 had been formed to smash the threat from the left but more often than not acted as a self-imposed police force on the right. For some reason Parrish received no retributions for his crime.

Skrewdriver Services had a rather blotted history. Trusting as he was, Ian allowed people free reign of it. The bands mail order outlet had never been hit by anything as bad as what Parrish had managed to do, but other organisers had fallen foul on the way. The Parrish incident was a prime case of a low achiever being unable to deal with money he would not normally have been able to make in legitimate ways. The temptation was just too great.

The previous organisers to Parrish were Kev and Roy Johnson from Harlow. Earlier that year the brothers had spent some time in jail and received fines totalling one-thousand five-hundred pounds. Pleading guilty at Chelmsford Crown court the Johnson's admitted inciting racial hatred by selling various pieces of merchandise for Skrewdriver Services. Under their control the Services had amassed a big line in racist badges, records, videos and T-shirts. After receiving some American extremist shirts through the post, they were visited by CID who had tracked the delivery and were watching their every move. One of the shirts, a caricature of Bart Simpson with a Swastika armband giving a Nazi salute, had been withdrawn in the States after threats of a copyright lawsuit.

Not too many people got a mention in Ian's songs with the exception of Patrick Harrington, but Parrish got the treatment in a song titled Renegade.

*We're gonna bring you down, bring you down*
*Bring you down to the ground*
*Because you're a renegade, how much did you get paid*
*For robbing your comrades and running away*
*You're a renegade, Is Judas your name?*
*One day we will find you - you're a renegade*

*If we knew then what we know now*
*You'd never have the chance to steal*
*But I tell you now what the future will hold*
*One day those tears will be real*

The tears that Ian referred to are the tattoos on Neil Parrish's face. Parrish was the kind of man that would blow his booty on beer and rubbish. He probably spent the money within a matter of weeks and then regretted that he had burned his bridges leaving no way back. The life he'd known as a Skinhead for almost all of his adult life was all he knew. The candle had been burnt at both ends and left him with nothing. Outside of the Skinhead world he was anonymous, empty and lost. As far as everyone was concerned he was a marked man.

Generally, Nineteen ninety-two was a bad year, and if, like the Chinese, Blood and Honour had to give it a name, it would probably be 'the year of treachery'. As if Crane and Parrish was bad enough another kick in the teeth was just around the corner.

Due to the recent boom in Germany, Blood and Honour were keen to be involved and thus set up a new division 'Blut und Ehre'. Financed in Britain, the magazine was almost solely made up of the British edition translated into German. They had their own merchandise outlet and filing system. Everything coming to England for them was forwarded on to their base near Hamburg. After collecting money for merchandise and sales of their magazine, their organiser disappeared with the loot. Although he ventured to South Africa to join the AWB in their violent struggle with the enemies of Apartheid, he was still guilty of stealing his comrades money. According to the law of Blood and Honour, no matter what he did in South Africa he would not be redeemed for his betrayal in Europe.

Among the publicity for the launch of Virgin Radio was a list of groups that were banned from the station's airwaves. Among those on the forbidden list was the name Skrewdriver. It was no surprise to Ian, it had been a long time since he celebrated in a West end pub at the airing of his specially recorded session for John Peel's Radio One evening show. How he would have loved to have been up there with his idols the Rolling Stones. In a rare in-depth interview Ian told Last Chance "I would like to have made a lot of money and been on Top of the pops. What other person that's ever been in a band wouldn't. I would never have changed my songs just for the fame though."

There is no doubting that, had Ian taken a different course, he may well have made it big in the world of Pop music. Ian had almost single handedly dragged Skinhead music through the narrow confines of Punk and onto a broader Rock based spectrum. Even many of his critics could not deny a sparkle of talent in the eyes of a man they grew to detest. If Ian had a change of heart and turned his back on his racist views there would have cer-

tainly been a queue of people waiting to sign him up, if not for his talent then for his conversion. The controversy would have certainly shifted some records. It would have been the one death blow that would have finished off the RAC scene in one full swoop. Ian was an idealist and as if married to his cause he would see it through in sickness and in heath and for richer or poorer. A man in his position could not easily divorce himself from his position as leader of the Skins. For his die hard following he would always be the original Skinhead who never sold out.

Skrewdriver Services was again up and running. Not wanting the work load, Ian had passed it on to a local activist in Heanor. A division of the services was also set up in Germany to meet the demand of the worlds biggest market for skinhead wares. A new line of shirts and Compact disks were on sale. Included in the new additions was the second Ballads CD, Our Time will come. With a more professional sound than the previous one,

Ian had concentrated heavily on melody and had even enlisted some female backing vocals on two of the tracks. 'Another prayer for the dying', 'Wasted life' and 'Left to drown' were all representative of Ian's dismay at what he saw as a decaying nation awaiting it's death. The title track saved the listener from submerging into a feeling of depression. Ian never gave up hope that how ever far things went, his race and nation would be saved from the abyss.

# Chapter Twenty-Four
# Under the Cosh

With Blood and Honour ending Nineteen ninety two in the headlines, the organisation found itself being criticised from all quarters. This was nothing new, but what was disturbing for Ian was some corners of the nationalist movement were also getting in on the act. Colin Jordan, to whom Ian referred to as 'the fool on the hill', was writing a book, National vanguard, about the prospects for modern day Nationalists. Although still very much respected by many nationalists, Jordan's vision was one not shared by the Skinheads. Jordan wanted non-drinkers, grey in appearance, but fanatical in their love for Hitler. On Skinheads he retorted "It is a mistake to disregard the fact that there is some good in some Skinheads, who at least are prepared to have a go. It is an even bigger mistake to discount the fact that there is much that is very bad in Skinheads."

Colin Jordan was seen as an idealist and Ian respected that, but in his view the man had lost all sense of reality. The British public were not going to be won over by long winded lectures and the sort of self-discipline that befalls the strictest religious cults. Young people want music, fun, drinking and partying, and if Ian could instil a political direction within it then this, in his view, would serve the cause in a far greater way.

Both had yet to achieve what they had really set out to do, but Ian was certainly the closest. It was only a lack of investment and the media's condemnation that had stopped him building a large un-crushable movement, the likes of what black rappers have achieved. Jordan on the other hand was surrounded by a very small clique of fanatics prepared to live like Nazi monks. Their appeal for a wholesome return to old values would attract a few people, but many were simply lonely lost souls with nothing in their lives, searching for a future. Jordan's was a language that was outdated. In a world of bright colours and fast moving life styles, Jordan was being left behind. This was also, in some part, due to a lack of funds. Black and white typed documents and newsletters were unlikely to pull in a people used to the gloss of flashy magazines and twenty-four hour TV channels. In media terms it was like selling a mini car to Rolls Royce owners.

Ian Stuart had a far better understanding of the physics of recruitment. Jordan had failed to see the importance of getting the foot in the door. Just as a salesmen will struggle over his first few minutes at the door before gaining his targets confidence enough to go in for the kill. Perhaps the mistake of Skrewdriver, and Rock Against Communism in general, was its extremity. If they had worked their politics in a more patriotic manner perhaps they could have received a greater return. This worked for Ultima-Thule in Sweden who made millions from their 'Viking Rock'. The group were all ex-nationalist Skinheads, but portrayed themselves not as Nazis, but as Swedish patriots. They were in some part disowned by some Swedish Skinheads, but gained a massive audience of ultra-patriotic youth who were ripe for the kind of 'Sweden for Swedish' sentiments of the Scandinavian Right. The group found enemies in the media, but it didn't stop them getting to number one in the national charts, something Skrewdriver could only dream of.

With attendances increasing it was becoming harder to organise RAC concerts. The large venues were not easy to bluff and difficult to secure. Usually a word from the police, or violent threats from the left, was enough for the venue owners to renege on the deal. A remedy would have to be found.

The East Midlands was made up of small towns, villages and sprawling countryside. Small towns were easily cut off by the police, demonstrators would have little problem inflicting problems on would-be concert organisers and the same went for villages. The countryside was perhaps the answer. Just as in the mid-eighties in Suffolk, The organisers would find a farmer sympathetic enough to allow his farm to become an outside musical Neurenberg rally. For the right price, The right price being one thousand pounds.

Selston, a small farming valley on the borders of Nottinghamshire and Derbyshire, was the venue of the European Aryan Festival. The farm had previously been hired out as a venue for Raves and so could handle the kind of event planned.

Unlike the Waterloo gig, publicity for the Euro Aryan Fest was by mail order and word of mouth in an attempt to avoid the kind of clashes and trouble that the RAC fans had endured in London. Instructions were given to avoid the courtship of the media. It was felt that large numbers could be achieved without the hassle. At a concert the week before, staged at The Portland pub in Jacksdale, leaflets were given out explaining where the re-direction points would be. Only a handful of people knew where the festival site was, and even Ian was kept in the dark about the locality.

If the national press hadn't caught on to the idea, then the same couldn't be said about the police, who were given strict instruction to locate the venue. They had gone to extreme lengths in their search, hiring a spotter plane to photograph every farm in the Nottinghamshire and Derbyshire area.

Work on the stage and arena started a week prior to the festival, with six men putting up scaffolding, connecting the trailers and covering the outskirts of the farm with sheets, so as to avert prying eyes. During this work one of the men, Benny, was on his way to the farm when he spotted police loading up a blue arctic lorry with the ten thousand cans of lager that had been stored in a barn. His heart sank. He knew that they were on to it but hadn't bargained on this. "You'd never seen so many coppers in your life, there was Notts and Derby police swarming the place. You'd have thought there was drugs in there or some maniac shooting at people. It was unbelievable."

The day after the raid, Benny received a knock on the door. It was the police, there to serve a writ against him and the other two main organisers. Ian also got the treatment, even though he'd had nothing to do with the organisation of the event.

The police told Benny that they were expecting five hundred Left-wing anarchists from Germany who were coming over for the single purpose of a violent clash. In Germany the press were quoting the Anarchists and referring to the festival as 'the bloodbath'.

The documents from the High court of Justice claimed there was 'a substantial potential for public disorder'. The technicality of the whole thing was that no-one had informed the police or local authority and a licence to hold such an event had not been sought. One of the leaflets advertising the festival had the entrance fee of twelve pounds printed on it. For this reason they could not claim that it was simply a party in which a licence was not required. In any event it was quite likely that the police would have gone to any measure to stop the festival taking place. The technicality was just a sign of the way that the law works against amateurs oblivious to the legal requirements.

The police warned Ian, Benny and Adi that if they were seen congregating with five or more people in the Notts-Derby area they would be immediately arrested. Ian was fuming, yet again the might of the government was standing in his way. It made his blood boil when he realised that it had started from the initial word of an Anti-Nazi League activist who'd set up a counter demonstration in Heanor. In their press release the ANL called for all pubs

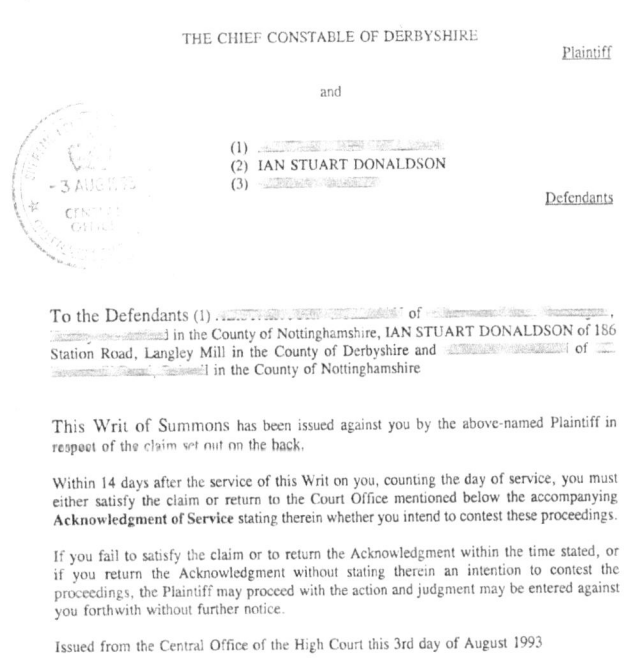
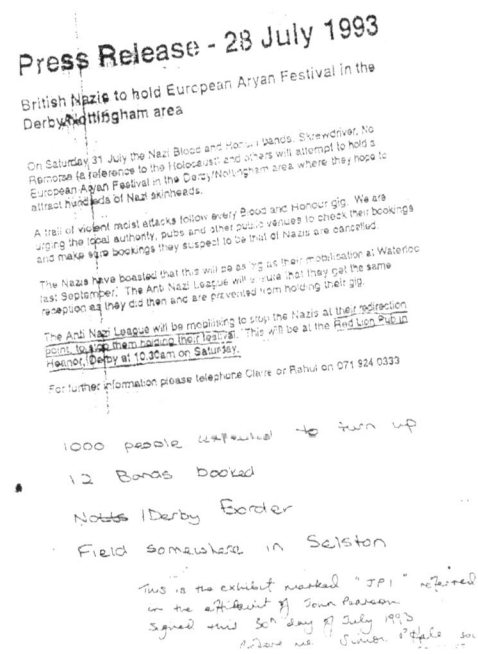

and public venues to check their bookings and cancel any suspect events. "The Anti-Nazi League will ensure they are prevented from holding their gig." On the day they managed to mobilise about a hundred demonstrators in Heanor, almost all of them bussed-in from London.

Thirty-first of July arrived and bore witness to the biggest Notts-Derby police operation since the Miners strikes of the early eighties. The entire police campaign cost the tax payer half a million pounds. There were road blocks set up at three junctions on the M1 motorway, vetting cars as they came off the slip roads. Selston was sealed off, and although they'd put paid to the festival there, the police still feared that a secondary venue would emerge enabling the festival to go ahead. Helicopters were scrambled to check on the area and specifically spot any movement from the Skinheads.

The Notts and Derby police, well known to hate each other, spent the best part of their day exchanging insults. The bad feeling generally stemmed from the fact that the Derbyshire constabulary was the poorer of the two, and while they drove around in F registration cars, their Nottinghamshire counterparts swanned around in newer J reg. models.

Ian headed for Porkys, a pub in Burton on Trent, Staffordshire. Once there, Ian arranged a small gig with top German Skin-band Noie Werte. The performances of both groups were super-charged with Ian laying into the police from his position on stage. Porky's was a small venue and so only about two hundred of the expected two thousand actually got to see their heroes in action. On top of this they were deeply out of pocket. They had done what they could but it was nothing short of a disaster. As if to rub salt into their wounds, the organisers read in the following days press that a young man had died at an illegal Rave held in the same area as the proposed Aryan Fest. Another open air event in the vicinity had been held by gipsies. They too had failed to acquire the correct licences but had gone about their business un-bothered by a police force concerned only with the movements of the young Nationalists.

If questions were asked after Waterloo, there were certainly some to be answered here. Primarily, which way now?

# Chapter Twenty-Five
# Time to Die

*Live your life to the full - Never say die*
*Keep on breaking rules up until the end*
*Don't let nobody tell you what to do*
*In the end the decision's up to you*
*Live life to the full*
*It'll soon be Time to Die*

In the Midlands things that he had avoided in London were starting to catch up with Ian. Local police would, on occasion, follow him from Pub to Pub at the weekends. There was a campaign by Mansfield based Marxists to bar him from Rock City in Nottingham. Ian's local, the Red Lion in Heanor, was closed down at a time when MP's were calling on police to crack down on licensees who allow their premises to be used by subversive groups. Again it felt as if he was under seige with nowhere to run.

The last couple of years had seen Ian move in with his fiancee Diane. It was very much an on-off affair, and there was never really any talk of a Wedding, although it was probable that it may happen one day. Children, on the other hand, was a completely different matter. Ian had shown no signs of wanting to start up his own family. It may well have been out of fear of his own fate or the un-steadiness of his relationship. Would it be fair to bring a child into a life so ravaged by turmoil and uncertainty? Ian thought not, although he did enjoy the visits he made to various nationalist fami-

lies in the area. The picture painted of him in the media was very different from the one his close friends knew. Sure he was a determined and politically committed man, but he always had time for friends and fans alike. Many people were surprised by his generosity and friendliness, of course this hand of comraderie was only outstretched to white folks and not those whose political persuasion was a hue of deep red.

Blood and Honour had certainly been through the wars of late, under the cosh by the establishment, under constant pressure from the left and at the mercy of some less than honourable members of their own movement. The setbacks of Waterloo and Nottingham could not easily be forgotten, nor too could the deaths of four RAC musicians who were killed instantly when their car went out of control on the M4 motorway near Bath. The band, Violent Storm, were on their way to the airport where they were to join friends and fly to Valencia, Spain, where a RAC Festival was being held.

The scene in Spain was similar to many on the continent that were springing up almost everywhere. Gone were the confines of old Fascist party barriers, replaced by radical splinter groups with a heavy understanding of street music, as well as street violence. Groups like 'Action Radical' in Valencia would organise around a network of fanzines. Funds were drawn from merchandise sales. Every self-respecting racist must have a Celtic Cross flag, a Skrewdriver T-shirt and a copy of Mein Kampf written in their native tongue. With the money from these sales, added to the smaller amounts from fanzine subscriptions, they may just have enough to stage a concert. Local bands were popular but the real crowd pullers were groups from Britain. The bands themselves would not earn much but would be allowed to gain a holiday in a place that their personal budgets would often fail to reach. There was a different buzz about foreign gigs, to many Euro-racists it would be their only chance of seeing their pop heroes, and for some of the musicians the only chance to feel like pop idols.

In Britain it was not all doom and gloom for the Right. The BNP were gaining a foothold in East London and their profile around the country was higher than ever before. With the National Front out of the picture and bickering their way into obscurity, the BNP remained the one last political bastion of the mainstream Right. Many of their events were supported by Blood and Honour Skinheads, much to the embarrassment of their leader John Tyndall, who needed their strength on the street but generally hated the sight of them. No-one could argue that Skinheads could be good for your public image, but the situation wasn't as straight forward as that. Many Skinheads had more guts than their longer haired counterparts.

The people of the Eastend seemed oblivious to the reputation the BNP had amassed in the media. As far as they were concerned they were the only ones speaking out for the disenfranchised whites. All the major parties were clamouring for the ever-growing immigrant vote, Somalians and Bengali's seemed to be jumping the housing queues and when complaints were made, the Eastenders would find that the faces of the councillors and government representatives were, more often than not, black in colour. Young Asians had discarded their passive image and were gaining a name for themselves on the tough Eastend streets. The violence was explosive, culminating in the stabbing of a young boy in his school classroom. There was anger and the BNP were keen to exploit it. They infiltrated local demonstrations as well as holding their own. The whole situation was a veritable tinder box waiting to go boom.

Ian was not keen on Tyndal, but had time for some of their members and respected the party's conventional nationalist political stance. On Friday Seventeenth of September Ian phoned Benny, he was in an upbeat mood and had some news that was sure to please his comrade. "The BNP won their seat in the Isle of Dogs." It was all over the newspapers. The Sun's headline 'Racist party wins first seat', and Breakfast TV's shots of minor skirmishes between BNP Skinheads and Anti-Nazi League activists had Ian captivated. The BNP had gained a massive amount of credibility and if they could capitalise on it then they would make one of the biggest breakthroughs for the right-wing since the heyday of the National Front in the mid-seventies. All the squabbles and personality clashes were almost forgotten overnight. The racist Right had a victory to celebrate. Many ardent followers of Fascism would spend hours ranting on about the final victory and how tomorrow belongs to them, but I bet even a few of them would have pinched themselves to see if it was all really happening. It had been so long since they'd really had something in black and white to crow about, other than a few violent victories smashing the Left. The ardent struggle to impregnate the barriers stopping them from achieving any kind of political credibility had lost them many an activist. Years of slugging it out, dodging the police and fighting the opposition had left them with a hard-core band of fanatics, but here they were in the midst of their toughest times celebrating a political victory. It was proof to many that no matter how bad the situation in the country was - victory was always possible. The will of a people is a very powerful thing. A week later the Right would be raising their glasses for a very different reason.

On the morning of Thursday, Twenty-third of September Nineteen ninety-three, Benny received a phone call. It was Ian asking if he'd be able to see him that day. Benny explained that he'd better not come round as the police had phoned and were on their way to discuss the confiscated beer from the Euro Aryan Fest. He asked about the evening and said he intended to go to a Bikers pub near to him called The Durham Fox. Benny said he couldn't, but he'd promise to see him the following day. In the evening Ian met up with Cat, Dickie, a Skinhead called Boo, and a ginger haired fellow by the name of Rob. The five of them took Ian's car to Burton where they'd meet up with a couple of local Skins and have a drink at the Royal Oak in the Market Square. There was nothing particularly different about this evening, to his friends Ian was not only their inspirational leader he was also good fun to be around and enjoyed a good laugh. The lads decided to call it a day just before eleven, their was a gig planned for the following Saturday and still a fair bit to organise.

Rob hadn't been drinking so he took command of the car and the five sped off back along the A38 to Heanor. They had just overtaken a car, on a stretch of road near the Toyota factory in Burnaston, and were moving back into the nearside lane at about fifty five miles an hour, when suddenly something happened. The steering wheel lost control and suddenly the car was heading for the central reservation. Ian grabbed the wheel saying to Rob "Don't try and kill me I've got a gig on Saturday." There didn't seem to be any real danger and the comment was said as more of a joke, than out of fear. The next thing they knew the car had swung back across the road onto the grass verge spinning over and finally smashing into a ditch. It happened so quick. Cat, still dazed from the crash, said "What's happened here?" the seriousness of the incident was not ringing through. Gathering his wits about him, he looked over at his brother Dickie and said to Rob, who'd just come round, "He's in trouble." He then glanced around at the others. Immediately he said "Boo's dead." They both looked at Ian and the full extent of what had happened began to dawn on them. "Fuckin' hell" Cat blurted. Positioned in the middle of the back seat, with Dickie on the right and Boo to his left, Cat had endured the accident more successfully than his friends. The impact had penetrated the left side of the VW Polo where both Ian and Boo had sat.

BCM BOX 8514, LONDON WC1N 3XX.

The emergency services arrived and the lads were taken straight to hospital. All bar Boo, real name Stephen Flint, who was pronounced dead at the scene of the incident. Ian was rushed to Queens medical Centre in Nottingham, with severe head injuries. There he failed to regain consciousness and died at twenty minutes to eleven on the Friday morning.

IAN STUART

FOREVER IN OUR HEARTS

That Friday morning Benny went to work as usual at the Coal delivery company. He met his friend 'Whitey' and told him of a strange phone call he'd received the previous evening and said he thought Boo was in trouble. Cat's girlfriend Mel had phoned him asking for Boo's address. "I could hear police radios in the background and thought he was in some kind of trouble." They phoned Boo's wife Paula, but she said she'd heard nothing, but Boo hadn't come back. Benny and his colleague got back to loading the lorry when a lad came running out of the office towards them. The lad looked a bit shaken. "You'd better put down the bags of coal and come and have a fag or something" he stammered. Benny enquired as to what the problem was. He stood in complete shock and the pair of them burst into tears when the lad said "Boo's dead." Benny had known Boo from school and he also worked with them on the Coal. The pain grew deeper as thoughts rushed through his brain. What of Boo's little kids, and his wife? The lad from the office continued and said that there had been a car crash and Boo had been killed instantly and another was critical in Hospital. For some reason Benny thought of Cat. Perhaps because it was his girlfriend who'd called the previous night. The two lads stood staring at each other in utter despair. It felt as if time had stood still. It was as if this somehow wasn't real. How they wished it wasn't. Clutching to a futile hope that it was all a bad dream. Someone shouted to Benny that his wife Tracy was on the phone. She delivered the news. "Ian's dead." It was too much to bare. "I almost collapsed on the floor. It was so terrible."

A few people had assembled at Cat's house. Cat had received minor injuries. Richie had serious neck injuries but was out of critical danger in Hospital. Rob, who was also at Cat's, had a broken arm. Rob was going through torture. Despair ripping through him like a knife through butter. Voice croaking, Rob said what he thought was on the mind of the others. "I'm the man who's going to go down in history for killing Ian Stuart. They're going to make a big thing about me being the hero who killed Ian." No-one blamed Rob, but that didn't stop him feeling almost suicidal.

At a social held in memory of both Ian and Boo, staged at a club in Sandyacre, Rob got up and explained what had happened. With streams of tears rolling down his face he told of how the car had gone out of control and that there was nothing he could do. It was a brave thing to do. He felt as if the whole place hated him, but yet courage told him that this was something he must do, not only for the people assembled, but for himself too.

As news got out about Ian's death, a chilling numbness fell across the nationalist world, engulfing all his many friends and fans. It was more than just the death of a rock star. To many he had become more than a pop icon. Ian Stuart was not just a major part of the Blood and Honour movement, he was the centre and key to it all. He had formed it and held it together for six years. What future did it really have without him?

Blood and Honour quickly produced a newsletter informing its supporters the world over that 'The king was dead'. For the young nationalists it was something akin to the death of J.F. Kennedy or Princess Diana. Supporters from all over the world were eager for news of the funeral or memorial concerts. One man in Sweden was willing to sell the entire contents of his house just so he could come and pay his respects.

Some people involved with Blood and Honour wanted a concert the following weekend, claiming that no-one would dare to challenge them and that anyone who turned up to picket would be torn from limb to limb. Combat 18 had other ideas, and moved in quickly saying they must wait for a big show in London that November. November eventually turned to January and left a feeling of anti-climax with a lot of Ian's followers.

Two days after Ian's death Celtic Warrior were staging a concert in Bristol and on hearing the news decided to use the event to pay tribute to Ian. Paul Burnley of No Remorse read out a statement on behalf of all the bands. This was followed by a Skrewdriver track 'Suddenly'. As soon as Ian's voice began singing the lines 'One day if Suddenly I'm forced to take my leave, will you still carry on with the things that we believe?' the place erupted in tears. It was one of many smaller events that were being staged around the world.

To begin with the media greeted the news with silence. MTV mentioned it on their news bulletins and it made small print in the national press. In the nationalist world tributes flooded in from every corner of the world. Gottfried Kussel, a major Nazi leader who had just begun a ten year prison sentence wrote 'His spirit will be born through times and areas of all those in the struggle. This will give him eternal life. He has been the one who has started to win the hearts of our new generation'. Kussel signed off with a quote from the Odinist bible 'The Edda'. 'People die, Clans pass. One thing I know that's eternal - deeds glory of action'. In California adverts were placed in his memory. From Brixton Jail, in London, BNP Skinhead 'Biggsy' wrote 'He lifted my spirit ten years ago when I first heard his music, and I've never looked back since'. It was typical of the Skinheads' response. His death was mentioned in every Nationalist periodical imaginable.

Before the exact facts were known rumours were circulating that it was the Secret Services that killed Ian Stuart. A supporter in Germany told people how she had been told that Ian was on a hit list of European Nazis that were to be targets of the Israeli Secret Service MOSSAD. It was also said that someone had previously tampered with Ian's car. Combat 18 were in such a hurry to claim he was murdered that they mis-spelt Skrewdriver, replacing the 'k' with a 'c' in their article titled 'Ian Stuart killed by Jews'.

Others on the RAC scene preferred to put the incident down to fate. Cat, who sustained injuries in the accident and was better placed than anyone to judge, dismissed the allegations and said "It was just a blow out. We were doing fifty-five miles an hour and the steering wheel just snatched and we turned over. It was as if someone up above had put their hand in the car and said 'come here'. Ian had lived for National Socialism, and died for it."

Others pointed to signs of his fate in his own work. Skrewdrivers' last album featured songs like 'Time to Die' and the whole tone of his voice seemed to have changed. Ian's vocals somehow sounded tired and perhaps a little distant. Statements he made in recent interviews also covered the subject of his own fate. Ian told Last Chance "In five years time I'll be in Prison or dead." With the best of his work behind him, was he fated to die a Nationalist hero? One thing was for sure, the Skinheads and young Nationalists the world over would forever have a martyr for their cause. No-one chooses to die, but Ian would have been pleased to think that he had become the eternal cult figure of Nationalist struggle to so many people. The Teddy Boys had Elvis, the Punks had Sid Vicious, and now the racists had their very own dead modern day pop icon to worship.

In Derby, Coroner Peter Ashworth added to the mystery of how the accident had happened when he told the inquest that there was "No rhyme or reason to what happened." This was backed up by the investigators report. PC Charles Chapman said "I can not arrive at a definite conclusion as to what had caused the accident."

As expected, the Left were gloating. AFA stated 'We hope this will be a major set back to fascists everywhere. We are unable to confirm whether dying in mortal combat with a steering wheel qualifies for admission to Valhalla'.

Of all the public obituaries The Guardian's 'A hate they could hum' was probably the most in-depth, covering his life and including pictures of Ian and Skrewdriver security. The four page article ended with a quote from a Skinhead interviewed at Heanor's Red Lion pub. "Ian'll do more against the Left dead than alive."

In Blackpool, Arthur Donaldson was coming to terms with his thirty-six year old son's death, just two years after the loss of his own wife. Immediately after the news broke, the Donaldson household was bombarded with phone calls from old friends of Ian's wanting to know details of the funeral. The newspapers were also relentless in their search for a story. Mr Donaldson told the local paper "I am frightened of answering the phone. The media have been ruthless."

The media was full of stories about the contemplation of clashes between Nazis and Left-wingers at Ian's funeral. This had a large bearing on the decision to hold a small family funeral. "Ian had his beliefs and he attracted enemies as well as friends. Police vetoed his gigs and now that Ian is dead people are drumming it all up again." Mr Donaldson was determined to avoid the whole thing being turned into a political circus. "This should be a quiet funeral with his family and not the scene of a demonstration."

Almost everyone seemed to heed Ian's fathers' wishes. There were about twenty people present on the fifth of October at Carleton Crematorium to witness the peaceful ceremony. Among the twenty or so present was Cat, Ian's fiancee Diane, his brother Tony and his life long friend, and original Skrewdriver drummer, Grinny. A fast life of living on the edge was put to rest at a crematorium, free of the trappings of Nationalism that had engulfed his life, and not unlike a regular commemorative ceremony.

# Chapter Twenty-Six
# Aftermath

*Over the Sea, it calls to me*
*Yesterday's gone, I'm all alone*
*The long boat it sails into the sunset*
*You've finally found your place to rest*

*Sleep well my brother, do not be afraid*
*I can see the Valkyrie*
*Take me with you, take me so far away*
*I can see the Valkyrie*

*Now you've joined the ranks of the fallen*
*Carried away by Valhalla's calling*
*All that you fought for and all that you love*
*Watch over me brother, guide from above*

Ian's death had brought disarray as well as heart ache. A movement that Ian held together had now become divided. There were at least three factions, the strongest being Combat 18 who moved in almost immediately and set up a rival Blood and Honour magazine. With their violent reputation even hardened Skinheads chose their words carefully, allowing the organisation to gain almost full control. Anyone who failed to support them could find themselves on the wrong end of a violent attack and see their character destroyed in print.

Over two thousand racists turned up in London in mid-January Nineteen ninety-four. They came to pay their last respects at a commemorative concert being staged in East London by Combat 18. Many had come from Europe and America hoping to see performances from almost all the remaining British RAC bands. Included on the bill was Skullhead, who were to re-form for the show, and Brutal Attack who were back after a break of nearly three years. Instead of attending a Nationalist extravaganza, most spent the evening dispersed all over London after the venue in Beacontree, Essex, had been tumbled by the Police and ordered to close its doors to the racists.

With financial opportunities to be made from Ian Stuart's back catalogue, Combat 18 set up ISD Records. All compact disks produced were done so at a minimal cost, much the same as Rock-o-rama had done, but ISD would have the added bonus of paying no record-

## Euro-Nazis in gig riot

NEO-Nazis from Europe were involved in a series of weekend clashes in London, it was claimed last night.

They were here for a concert by Right-wing band Blood and Honour at an East End pub.

The gig was cancelled by police – and seven officers were injured trying to stop clashes between fascists and Left-wingers.

Nine people are due in court today on assault, affray and public order charges.

ing fees or royalties. After the expense of producing the CD's, at no more than one pound per disk, all else was profit. ISD even managed to obtain a copy of the recording of the forthcoming Hail Victory album by Skrewdriver. Their version of the CD was out before the official Rock-o-rama copy.

Herbert Egoldt had become a millionaire almost solely on the profit of Skrewdriver recordings, but was rich enough to allow this piracy to go unchallenged. After Ian's death Egoldt had contacted his father to discuss royalties but failed to send even one cheque to the Donaldsons. Likewise ISD wasn't interested in honouring their dead hero's estate. Ian's father gave a heavy sigh while discussing the subject, but felt that what he had never known he would never miss. Ian's political career was his alone, and although his brother was in awe of Ian, his father had never been at all interested. The sigh was not out of any financial loss to himself, but at the fact that just as in his life he was now being exploited after his death.

Resistance records inquired as to the possibility of producing a 'best of' compilation CD. The idea was still on the drawing board when Resistance boss, George Hawthorne, received a call from C18 warning him off. No-one would be allowed to move in on their lucrative income. Anyone who questioned where the money was going was given the treatment. One person who refused to toe the line answered a knock on his door to find Combat 18 hench men standing there with a machete in their hands. After having the blade held to his throat he suddenly saw things in a different light and promptly left the RAC scene, never to be seen again.

More and more people on the Blood and Honour circuit found themselves on the wrong end of this kind of threat, resulting in their numbers dropping vastly. Unlike their success with the National Front, Rock Against Communism's enemies had never been able to agitate splits in the movement, and yet it was now being torn apart from within. The one man who could stop the rot was gone.

England was no longer the pivotal nation of white power music in the world. Scandinavia was the new focal point, with Germany coming in a close second. It wasn't long before bands such as No Remorse lost heart and gave up. In terms of a Nationalist music scene, Britain had become a veritable ghost town. Most of the remaining bands, such as Brutal Attack and Squadron, chose to play abroad rather than in the UK. Most concerts in Britain required sanction from Combat 18. On approval bands were generally encouraged to donate their earnings to 'the cause'.

For a short while after Ian's death, there was talk of Skrewdriver re-forming with another singer. The idea was soon discarded as most people felt it was impossible to have a Skrewdriver without Ian Stuart. Skrewdriver minus Ian Stuart is equivalent to the Rolling

Stones without Mick Jagger. It would never work, He was Skrewdriver, there could be no other.

Stigger went on to form his own group, but although their set was made up mainly of Skrewdriver songs, he never really had the personality to carry it off, and the group eventually fell by the wayside. On a more successful venture, Stigger teamed up with Ken Mclellan from Brutal Attack, to produce the 'Pride' CD. Musically the recording was a great achievement for Stigger after the disappointing White Diamond and Strong Survive efforts that had his unique, but powerless, guitar sound stamped over them. If Stigger had previously failed to shine on guitar he certainly made up for it with 'Pride', but it was his vocals on a stirring tribute to Ian Stuart entitled 'Sleep well my brother' that had really caught the imagination.

Almost every Skinhead band was busy penning their own tributes. Some were better than others, many were lacking a certain something that had always kept them ranks apart from Skrewdriver in their standing. Among the more astute tributes were Brutal Attack's 'Last day of Summer' and No Remorse's 'Farewell Ian Stuart'.

*Farewell to a comrade, farewell to a friend*
*You did your best, shone above the rest*
*You were a white man 'till the end*
*Farewell Ian Stuart, a man we held so high*
*You will live forever, because heroes, heroes never die*

*From '82 we looked to you*
*To lead the movement and build the scene*
*Your white power songs, could never be wrong*
*You were the best band I've ever seen*
*Through all the years, the laughs and the beers*
*And the friends you made on the way*
*The times in a cell, when they gave you hell*
*From the course you never did stray*
*Against the Police and the Reds, and the traitors that fled*
*You stood up and took on the world*
*From the bedsits and digs, to the rallies and gigs*
*So proudly the flag you unfurled*
*And we will carry on with the hope in your songs*
*To turn back now would be such a sin*
*And we are ready to toil, for the blood and the soil,*
*Ian Stuart, you know we will win*

Ian Stuart will be remembered by his enemies as a man who used pop music to spread his evil message. To others he will always be a street-rock legend. Skrewdriver was a phenomenon that earned a cult status due to its uncompromising stance and appetite for youth rebellion. At a time when rock'n'roll was choking on its own worn out cliches, and its mentors were attempting to save the world from the heart of their mansions and recording studios, Skrewdriver were going where no-one had gone before. Ian Stuart kept punk rebellion alive by replacing the mainly manufactured calls of anarchy, with the stark and very real call of 'White Power'. Never has anyone fused politics with popular music to such a degree. For many white working class youths Ian Stuart was their leader, his songs were their bat-

tle cries and his albums their manifesto's. His audience was mostly made up of young people who genuinely felt that, for whatever reason, life, and more importantly society, had passed them by. The brutal education of street life had taught them to look after number one. In Ian Stuart they found a man who could give them their dreams, provide them with an identity of their own and give them a forum for their views.

Ian Stuart had not only inspired a generation of racist musicians in Britain, but his struggle was being repeated by young Nationalists all over the world. The success of Resistance records in America and Midgaard in Sweden can be traced back to Skrewdriver who supplied the songs that many Resistance bands emulated or covered at their gigs. In

Nineteen ninety-four a tremendously successful memorial concert was staged in Winsconsin, by Resistance. All the top U.S. groups appeared, along with guests from Europe and Australia. This was followed up with a double CD featuring twenty bands who recorded some of Ian Stuart's music in tribute of him. The leaders of Resistance read the situation carefully. Musically the U.S. scene was very different from Europe. Resistance attempted to move away from the kind of rock music Skrewdriver played, in favour of a faster metal sound that was more representative of the American music scene. This stance drew the attention of some very big players in the U.S. music industry. This change in direction was hailed a success when many U.S. Rock-based radio stations began playing tracks from Rahowa's 'Cult of the Holy War' CD and various songs by Bound for Glory.

From relatively humble beginnings to rock'n'roll death, Ian Stuart's was a life story akin to a stereotypical twentieth century rebel. The only thing that stood him apart from the likes of James Dean, Elvis Presley and Kurt Cobain, was politics and the wealth that it restricted him from. He had tasted fame and, although he found his efforts suppressed, his hunger never waned. Wanting so much to make it paused many problems for Ian. The music industry was dead against him, and yet he wanted to be there at the top. The more they criticised him the less likely he was going to be able to fit in those circles, yet the cold shoulder treatment wasn't leading him away from it. Every time they would knock him down the more determined he would become. RAC came as a release. In the early eighties the Skinhead scene was ripe for picking. The Skinheads had become more politicised than ever before and Ian recognised that it wouldn't take much to create a youth culture in which he would remain numero uno. Skinhead life and it's Nationalistic influences made it easy for the Skinheads to appreciate Ian's struggles with the music industry. There were many parallels drawn between Ian's treatment in the pop world and the Skinheads' struggles with society.

If Ian Stuart had been a talentless bore then it's probable that Skrewdriver would never have made it on to vinyl. The fact that they did last the pace is testament to a band that struggled more than any other in the history of popular music. Perhaps it was the struggle itself that kept the whole thing rolling. If the music media hadn't driven it underground perhaps it would have died the death of a short lived fashion phase.

Any group that breaks away from society is always going to be a danger. The more it is attacked, the more it rebels and establishes its own identity. The further away it gets, the harder it becomes to stop.

The police and authorities have gone to great lengths in their attempts to stop the likes of Blood and Honour, and although some action has been successful in stopping some individuals, it has failed to crush the movement. No matter who you are, or where you are from, when your back's against the wall you have two choices - fight or die. It is this mentality that allowed Skrewdriver to become, in Nationalist terms, the biggest thing since Adolf Hitler. Just as Ian Stuart prophesied in Nineteen ninety-one, "You'll have to kill me to stop me."

# Discography

**Singles**     **Skrewdriver**
You're so Dumb                          Chiswick  1977
Anti-Social                             Chiswick  1977
Built up, Knocked down                  TJM  1979
Back with a Bang                        Boots & Braces  1982
White Power                             White Noise  1983
Voice of Britain                        White Noise  1983
This Is White Noise (1 Track)           White Noise  1984
Invasion                                Rock-o-rama  1985
Johnny Joined the Klan (12")            Rock-o-rama  1988

**The Klansmen**

The Showdown                            White Pride  1989

**Albums**      **Skrewdriver**
All Skrewed Up                          Chiswick  1977
Hail the New Dawn                       Rock-o-rama  1985
Blood & Honour                          Rock-o-rama  1986
White Rider                             Rock-o-rama  1987
We've got the Power (Live)              Viking  1988
After the Fire                          Rock-o-rama  1988
Warlord                                 Rock-o-rama  1989
The Early Years Vol 1&2                 Rock-o-rama  1989
The Strong Survive                      Rock-o-rama  1990
Live & Kicking                          Rock-o-rama  1990
Freedom, What Freedom?                  Rock-o-rama  1992
Hail Victory                            Rock-o-rama  1994

**Ian Stuart**
No Turning Back                         Rock-o-rama  1988
Slay the Beast                          Rock-o-rama  1990
Patriot                                 Rock-o-rama  1991
Patriotic Ballads                       Rock-o-rama  1991
Justice for the Cottbus Six             Rock-o-rama  1992
Our Time Will Come                      Rock-o-rama  1993

# Discography

**The Klansmen**
Fetch the Rope              Rock-o-rama  1988
Rebel With a Cause          Rock-o-rama  1989
Rock'n'roll Patriots        Rock-o-rama  1991

**White Diamond**
The Reaper                  Rock-o-rama  1991
The Power and the Glory     Rock-o-rama  1993

**Compilation Albums**
Catch a Wave                Chiswick  1978
Long shots, Dead Certs
  & odds on Favourites      Chiswick  1978
United Skins                Boots & Braces  1982
No Surrender                Rock-o-rama  1985
No Surrender 2              Rock-o-rama  1986
No Surrender 3              Rock-o-rama  1988
Gods of War                 Rock-o-rama  1988
Gods of War 2               Rock-o-rama  1989
No Surrender 3              Rock-o-rama  1990
Gods of War 3               Rock-o-rama  1990
No Surrender 4              Rock-o-rama  1991
Gods of War 4               Rock-o-rama  1991

# Index

## A
ABH  56
Adam Douglas  57,59,60
Afflicted  125
Albert Marriner  53
Allen, Richard  9
Anderson, Ian  77
Andrew Brons  54,55
Andrew Benjamin  88,89,101,102,103,104
Angelic Upstarts  44,85,102,137
Anti-fascist action  85,131,137,155
Anti-nazi league  30,31,58,85,151
Armstrong, Roger  13,14,34
Aryan Nations  74

## B
Barker, Kirk  132,136
Battlezone  117
Benjamin, Andrew  88,89,101,102,
103,104
Birchill, Julie  20
Blaggers  137
Blair Peach  53
Bob Geldof  21
Boomtown Rats  21
Boots and Braces  75
Bovver Boots Agency  37,38
Bowie, David  26
Brons, Andrew  54,55
Burnley, Jon  80,124
Burnley, Paul  73,80,107,143,153
Bushell, Garry  39,46,47,52,68,69,70,81,
123,125
Buzzcocks  12

## C

Callendar, Garry  33
Carrol, Ted  13,28
Castles, Maurice  54,72
Cat  116,124,151,152,153,155
Celtic Dawn  117
Celtic Warrior  153
Charlie Seargent  68,106,141
Chiswick  12,13,14,15,16,17,22,23, 24,25,26,27,33,34
Clarke, Des  63,100,103
Close Shave  118
Cock Sparrer  41
Colin Jordan  91,146
Combat 18  106,141,153,154,156,157
Combat 84  46,51,59,106
Crane, Nicky  39,58,59,100,125,126,127, 128,129
Cross, Martin  81,119
Cutdown  89,100,102,103,104

## D

Dave Lozon  84,85
David Bowie  26
Derrick Holland  71,74,77,78,83
Des Clarke  63,100,103
Deutsche Alternative  122
Die-Hards  56
Dirlewanger  83,133
Douglas, Adam  57,59,60

## E

Effi  19,20
Egoldt, Herbert  86,96,157
Elvis Presley  79,80,109,160
English Rose  117
Enoch Powell  85

## F

Faith in the struggle  64,65,66

Flint, Steven  152
Four Skins  39,60
French, Mickey  40,42,44
Frenchy  41

## G

Garry Bushell  39,46,47,52,68,69,70,81, 123,125
Garry Callendar  33
Gately, Kevin  53
Geldof, Bob  21
Geoff Williams  41
George Hawthorne  138
George Lincoln Rockwell  91
Gerry Gable  71,72,73,87,103
Glenn Jones  33,35
Gordon Jackson  116,117
Gottfried Kussel  154
Grinny  8,11,12,20,31,32,33,34,35,70,155
Guns n'roses  138

## H

Harrington, Patrick  49,54,55,71,74,77, 78,79,83,86,101
Hartley, Ron  24
Hawthorne, George  138
Hells Angels  61
Herbert Egoldt  86,96,157
Holland, Derrick  71,74,77,78,83
Holmes, Murray  57

## I

Ian Anderson  77
Iggy Pop  23
Indecent Exposure  59,60

## J

Jackson, Gordon  116,117
Janet Street-Porter  22

Joe Hawkins  9
Joe Pearce  35,47,49,50,63,71,77,93
John Peel  25,26,27
John Tyndall  77,91,150
Johnny Reb  107
Johnny Quincy  31,33
Johnson, Kev  141
Jon Burnley  80,124
Jones, Glenn  33,35
Jordan,Colin  91,146
Julie Birchill  20

## K

Keith Thompson  139
Keith Moon  27
Ken Mclellan  75,78,80,99,100,107
Kev Johnson  141
Kevin Gately  53
Kevin McKay  11,19,33,35
Kev Turner  78,81,86
Kirk Barker  132,136
Ku Klux Klan  75,107,114,117
Kussel, Gottfried  154

## L

Lady Porter  87
Last Resort (Band)  39,41
Last Resort (Shop)  40,42,45,57
Lozon,Dave  84,85

## M

Madness  37,38,68,69,70
Malcolm Mclaren  12
Manor Park Royals  36
Mark Radcliffe  32
Marriner, Albert  53
Martin Cross  81,119
Mark Neeson  42
Marsh, Terry  137
Martin Smith  35

Martin Webster  71
Mathews, Robert  114,115
Maurice Castles  54,72
McGarry, Ross  106,114
McGowan, Shane  34
McKay, Kevin  11,19,33,35
McKay, Sean  11,12
Mclellan, Ken  75,78,80,99,100,107
Mickey French  40,42,44
Mick McAndrews  59
Mick Wall  28
Moon, Keith  27
Motorhead  13,33,34,111
Murray Holmes  57

## N

Neeson, Mark  42
Neil Parrish  117,139,140,141,142
New Order  34
Nicky Crane  39,58,59,100,125,126,127,
 128,129
Nine,Nine,Nine  20
No Remorse  73,78,80,95,96,103,105,
 119,133,153,157,158

## O

Ovaltinees  46,48,51,52,56

## P

Patrick Harrington  49,54,55,71,74,77,
 78,79,83,86,101
Pat Travis Band  25,27
Parrish, Neil  117,139,140,141,142
Parsons, Tony  136
Paul Burnley  73,80,107,143,153
Paul Swain  60
Peach, Blair  53
Pearce, Joe  35,47,49,50,63,71,77,93
Peel, John  25,26,27
Peter and the Wolf  46,52

Phil Walmsley 11,24,28,31,32,33
Powell, Enoch 85
Presley, Elvis 79,80,109,160
Public Enemy 59,60,112

## Q
Quincy, Johnny 31,33

## R
Radcliffe, Mark 32
Radikahl 138
Rahowa 137,160
Red action 52,72,85,99
Redskins 58,126
Resistance Records 138,160
Richard Allen 9
Robert Mathews 114,115
Rock-o-rama 57,62,77,81,83,86,
        89,91,95,112,113,138,157
Rockwell, George Lincoln 91
Roda, Steve 60
Roger Armstrong 13,14,34
Rolling Stones 8,11,43,111,143,158
Romantic Violence 84
Ron Hartley 24
Ross McGarry 106,114
Roxy 16,22,29

## S
Sammy Hagar Band 25,27
Scotty 45,49,50,57,60,76,96,107
Sean McKay 11,12
Seargent,Charlie 68,106,141
Sex Pistols 12,19,23,33,39
Sham 69 19,24,29,30,33
Shane McGowan 34
Skinhead Moonstomp 10,28
Skullhead 78,81,83,86,87,103
Stanley Park 17
Steven Flint 152

Steve Roda 60
Steve Strange 19
Stigger 114,119,158
Squadron 103,157
Smiley Jon 114
Smith, Martin 35
Splodgenessabounds 56
Sudden Impact 75,76,80,95
Suggs 22,26,34,35,37,38,68,69,70
Swain, Paul 60

## T
Ted Carrol 13,28
Teddy Boys 19,23
Terry Marsh 137
The Business 39,44
The Cavern 87,88
The Clash 22
The Damned 29
The Elite 41
The Jam 34
The Nipps 34
The Police 16,19,26
Thompson, Keith 139
Tony Parsons 136
Tony Wilson 34
Toy Dolls 56
Tumbling Dice 11,14
Turner, Kev 78,81,86
Tyndall, John 77,91,150

## U
Ultima Thule

## V
Vengeance 95
Virgin Radio 142
Violent Storm 87,150
Vortex 23,27,28

## W
Wall, Mick  28
Walmsley, Phil  11,24,28,31,32,33
Warlock  11
Webster, Martin  71
White Aryan Resistance  75
White Boss  36
Williams, Geoff  41
Wilson, Tony  34

## X
Xray Spex  23

# Distributors

*European distributor:*

**Midgård**
Box 220 27
400 72 Gothenburg
Sweden
www.midgaard.org

*North American distributor:*

**Panzerfaust**
PO Box 188
Newport, MN  55055
USA
www.panzerfaust.com

www.ingramcontent.com/pod-product-compliance
Lightning Source LLC
Chambersburg PA
CBHW060412010526
44107CB00006B/658